THE LEADERSHIP LIBRARY

Volume
10

Weddings, Funerals, and Special Events

Eugene H. Peterson
Calvin Miller
and others

Carol Stream, Illinois

WORD BOOKS
PUBLISHER
WACO, TEXAS

A DIVISION OF
WORD, INCORPORATED

WEDDINGS, FUNERALS, AND SPECIAL EVENTS

Introduction and ancillary copy ©1987 Christianity Today, Inc.

Chapter 1 ©1987 Eugene H. Peterson
Chapter 2 ©1987 Ken Wilson
Chapter 3 ©1983 Christian Century Foundation, reprinted by permission from
          the January 1983 issue of *The Christian Ministry*.
Chapter 4 ©1987 Bruce Rowlison
Chapter 5 ©1987 R. Kent Hughes
Chapter 6 ©1987 Rick McKinniss
Chapter 7 ©1987 Paul Walker
Chapter 8 ©1987 Calvin Ratz
Chapter 9 ©1987 Mark Coppenger
Chapter 10 ©1987 Roger F. Miller
Chapter 11 ©1987 Garth Bolinder
Chapter 12 ©1987 Calvin Miller
Chapter 13 ©1987 Paul Anderson
Chapter 14 ©1987 Cal LeMon

A LEADERSHIP/Word Book. Copublished by Christianity Today, Inc. and Word,
Inc. Distributed by Word Books.

Cover art by Joe Van Severen

Library of Congress Cataloging-in-Publication Data

Weddings, funerals & special events.

   (Leadership library ; v. 10)
   "A Leadership/Word book."
   1. Pastoral theology.   2. Occasional services.
I. Peterson, Eugene H., 1932-   II. Miller,
Calvin.   III. Title: Weddings, funerals, and
special events.   IV. Series.
BV4011.W34   1987   253   87-2044
ISBN 0-917463-13-7

Printed in the United States of America

THE LEADERSHIP LIBRARY
V O L U M E   1 0
WEDDINGS, FUNERALS, AND SPECIAL EVENTS

CONTENTS

75296

INTRODUCTION

No matter how much church ministry changes, some elements remain the same. For many centuries, pastors have performed weddings and officiated at funerals, baptisms, dedications, confirmations, and community events. Today, that role remains constant, but today's context forces ministers to continually reexamine their approach.

This book focuses on these public occasions where the "priestly" functions are required. How can pastors minister most effectively in these situations?

In keeping with the practical nature of THE LEADERSHIP LIBRARY, each chapter comes from a pastor who writes out of personal acquaintance with the struggles and successes of these ministries. These writers are candid about the possibilities and limitations of the pastor's role, and they base their reflections on specific instances.

Chapter 1 looks at the overriding question: What is the pastor's essential role in any of these public occasions? The thoughtful response is offered by Eugene H. Peterson, pastor of Christ Our King Presbyterian Church in Bel Air, Maryland.

Chapters 2 through 5 focus on weddings. Since the pastor is almost always involved with the couple before (and after) the wedding day, more is at stake than simply officiating at a ceremony.

How do we create a climate within the church that encourages lasting marriages? One congregation that has wrestled earnestly with this question is Emmaus Fellowship in Ann Arbor, Michigan. Pastor Ken Wilson explains their direct approach in chapter 2.

One of the often-strained situations every pastor faces is when a couple unrelated to the church wants to be wed in the church. Chapter 3 asks, "Should we marry the unchurched?" and Douglas G. Scott, rector of St. Martin's Church in Radnor, Pennsylvania, tells how he handles this delicate but potentially redemptive situation.

Techniques of effective premarital counseling are shared in chapter 4 by Bruce Rowlison, pastor of Gilroy (California) Presbyterian Church, who coauthored *Let's Talk about Your Wedding & Marriage* (Green Leaf Press, 1985).

And finally, what does a minister need to keep in mind for the rehearsal and actual wedding ceremony? In chapter 5, the important elements are reviewed by Kent Hughes, pastor of College Church in Wheaton, Illinois, and coauthor of *The Christian Wedding Planner* (Tyndale, 1984).

Chapters 6 to 10 deal with the pastor's role in funerals and the accompanying ministry to the grieving.

The first step is preparing a congregation to face that inevitable enemy, death. Rick McKinniss is pastor of Kensington Baptist Church in Kensington, Connecticut, but at the time he wrote this chapter, he was just finishing a pastorate at Emmaus Baptist Church in Northfield, Minnesota, where he saw firsthand the need to help a congregation get ready for death.

When death actually comes, what are the immediate steps a church should take? Paul Walker describes how he and the Mount Paran Church of God in Atlanta, Georgia, minister to the grieving.

Ministry during the actual funeral and graveside services is considered by Calvin Ratz, veteran pastor of Abbotsford (British Columbia) Pentecostal Assembly.

Then, two specific problem situations are addressed: "Funerals of Those You Barely Know" by Mark Coppenger, pastor of First Baptist Church in El Dorado, Arkansas, and "Handling the Hard Cases" — such tragedies as suicide, infant death, and victims of violence — written by Roger Miller, minister at the Central Christian Church in Jefferson, Iowa.

The last section of this volume describes some of the other special events over which pastors preside.

Infant baptisms and dedications provide a unique opportunity to minister to the family and the congregation, as Garth Bolinder explains from his perspective as pastor of Modesto (California) Covenant Church.

Calvin Miller, pastor of Westside Baptist Church in Omaha, Nebraska, writes about the obstacles he has to overcome in the baptism of adults.

Not all readers of this book will be involved in churches that practice confirmation, but Paul Anderson, pastor of Trinity Lutheran Church in San Pedro, California, points out the transferable principles that will help any church instill and confirm the faith for another generation.

Finally, Cal LeMon, pastor of Evangel Temple Christian Center in Springfield, Missouri, discusses the pastor's role as community spokesperson, whether the occasion is a banquet invocation, a baccalaureate address, or a newspaper column.

These public occasions become milestones in people's lives — and in our ministries. Each time of joy or grief opens people, if only for a moment, to pastors and to the divine realities they represent. And so these events deserve our continuing attention.

At a wedding, Jesus rejoiced. At a friend's graveside, Jesus wept. At both, he worked miracles. Jesus sensed these moments as dramas that held people's rapt attention. Through his ministry at these occasions, God became the leading actor.

That remains our present call.

— Marshall Shelley
Managing Editor
LEADERSHIP

ONE

THE MINISTRY OF CEREMONY AND CELEBRATION

One of the ironies of pastoral work is that on these occasions in our ministry when we are most visible — out in front giving invocations and benedictions, directing ceremonies, and delivering addresses — we are scarcely noticed.

EUGENE H. PETERSON

Pastors enter and embrace the totality of human life, convinced there is no detail, however unpromising, in people's lives in which Christ may not work his will. Pastors agree to stay with the people in their communities week in and week out, year in and year out, to proclaim and guide, encourage and instruct as God works his purposes (gloriously, it will eventually turn out) in the meandering and disturbingly inconstant lives that compose our congregations.

This necessarily means taking seriously, and in faith, the dull routines, the empty boredom, and the unattractive responsibilities that make up much of most people's lives. It means witnessing to the transcendent in the fog and rain. It means living hopefully among people who from time to time get flickering glimpses of the Glory but then live through stretches, sometimes long ones, of unaccountable grayness. Most pastoral work takes place in obscurity: deciphering grace in the shadows, searching out meaning in a difficult text, blowing on the embers of a hard-used life. This is hard work and not conspicuously glamorous.

But there are interruptions in this work, not infrequent, in which the significance blazes all of itself. The bush burns and is not quenched. Our work is done for us, or so it seems, by the event. We do nothing to get these occasions together: no prayer meeting, no strategic planning, no committee work, no altar call. They are given. They are redolent with meaning and almost always, even among unbelievers, evoke a sense of reverence. These interruptions of the ordinary become occasions of ceremony and celebration: weddings, funerals, baptisms and dedications, anniversaries and graduations, events at which human achievements are honored. Instead of deficiency of meaning, which characterizes so many lives and for which people compensate in frenzy or fantasy, there is an excess: the ecstasy of love, the dignity of death, the wonder of life, the nobility of achievement. These occasions burst the containers of the everyday and demand amplitude and leisure in which to savor the fullness. No love was ever celebrated enough, no death ever mourned enough, no life adored enough, no achievement honored enough. We set aside time, clear space, call friends, gather families, assemble the community. Almost always, the pastor is invited to preside and to pray.

But when we arrive we are, it seems, hardly needed, and in fact, barely noticed. One of the ironies of pastoral work is that on these occasions when we are placed at the very center of the action, we are perceived by virtually everyone there to be on the margins. No one would say that, of course, but the event that defines the occasion — love, death, birth, accomplishment — also holds everyone's attention. No one inquires of the pastor what meaning there is in this. Meaning is there, overwhelmingly obvious, in the bride and groom, in the casket, in the baby, in the honored guest.

The pastor is, in these settings, what the theater calls "fifth business" — required by the conventions but incidental to the action, yet, in its own way, important on the sidelines. This is odd, and we never quite get used to it; at least I never do. In the everyday obscurities in which we do most of our work, we often have the sense of being genuinely needed. Even when unnoticed, we are usually sure our presence makes a difference, sometimes a critical difference, for we have climbed to the abandoned places, the bereft lives, the "gaps" that Ezekiel wrote of (22:30), and have spoken Christ's Word and witnessed Christ's mercy. But in these situations where we are given an honored place at the table, we are peripheral to everyone's attention.

Where Is the Spotlight?

At weddings, love is celebrated. The atmosphere is luminous with adoration. Here are two people at their best, in love, venturing a life of faithfulness with each other. Everyone senses both how difficult and how wonderful it is. Emotions swell into tears and laughter, spill over into giggles, congeal into pomposity. In the high drama that pulls families and friends together for a few moments on the same stage, the pastor is practically invisible, playing a bit part at best. We are geometrically at the center of the ceremony, but every eye is somewhere else.

At funerals, death is dignified. The not-being-there of the deceased is set in solemn ritual. Absence during this time is more powerful than presence. Grief, whether expressed torrentially or quietly, is directed into channels of acceptance and gratitude that save it from wasteful spillage into regret and bitterness. The tears that blur perception of the living, including the pastor, clarify appreciation of the dead.

At the baptisms and dedications of infants, the sheer wonder of infant life upstages the entire adult world. The glory that radiates from the newborn draws even bystanders into praise. In the very act of holding an infant in the sacrament of baptism or the service of dedication, the pastor, though many times larger, stronger, and wiser, is shadowed by the brightness of the babe.

At anniversaries and graduations, ground breakings and inaugurations — the various community occasions when achievements are recognized and ventures launched — the collective admiration or anticipation produces a groundswell of emotion that absorbs everything else. Every eye is focused on, and every ear is tuned to, the person honored, the project announced, the task accomplished, the victory won. The pastor, even praying in the spotlight and with the amplification system working well, is not really in the spotlight.

And so it happens that on the occasions in our ministry when we are most visible — out in front giving invocations and benedictions, directing ceremonies, and delivering addresses — we are scarcely noticed.

The One Thing Needful

If no one perceives our presence the way we ourselves perceive it — directing operations, running the show — what is going on? We are at the margins during these occasions. No one came to see us. No one came to hear us. We are not at all needed in the way we are accustomed to being needed.

No one needs us to tell the assembled people that this moment of time partakes of eternity and that things of great moment are taking place. No one needs us to proclaim that this is a unique event, never to be repeated, in which we are all privileged participants. All this is unmistakably obvious and not to be missed by even the stiff-necked and uncircumcised of heart.

So why are we there? We are there to say *God*. We are there for one reason and one reason only: to pray. We are there to focus the overflowing, cascading energies of joy, sorrow, delight, or appreciation, if only for a moment but for as long as we are able, on God. We are there to say God personally, to say his name clearly, distinctly, unapologetically, in prayer. We are there to say it without hemming and hawing, without throat clearing and without shuffling, without propagandizing, proselytizing, or manipulating. We have no other task on these occasions. We are not needed to add to what is there; there is already more than anyone can take in. We are required only to say the Name: Father, Son, Holy Ghost.

All men and women hunger for God. The hunger is masked and misinterpreted in many ways, but it is always there. Everyone is on the verge of crying out "My Lord and my God!" if only circumstances push them past their doubts or defiance, push them out of the dull ache of their routines or their cozy accommodations with mediocrity.

On the occasions of ceremony and celebration, there are often many people present who never enter our churches, who do their best to keep God at a distance and never intend to confess Christ as Lord and Savior. These people are not accustomed to being around pastors, and not a few of them politely despise us. So it is just as well that we are perceived to be marginal to the occasion.

The occasions themselves provide the push toward an awareness of an incredible Grace, a dazzling Design, a defiant Hope, a courageous Faithfulness. But awareness, while necessary, is not enough. Consciousness raising is only prolegomena. Awareness, as such, quickly trickles into religious sentimentalism or romantic blubbering, or hardens into patriotic hubris or pharasaic snobbery. Our task is to nudge the awareness past these subjectivities into the open and say God.

The less we say at these times the better, as long as we say God. We cultivate unobtrusiveness so that we do not detract from the sermon being preached by the event. We must do only what we are there to do: pronounce the Name, name the hunger. But it is so easy to get distracted. There is so much going on, so much to see and hear and say. So much emotion. So much, we think, "opportunity." But our assignment is to the "one thing needful," the invisible and quiet center, God.

We do best on these occasions to follow the sermonic advice of the Rebbe Naphtali of Ropshitz: Make the introduction concise and the conclusion abrupt — with nothing in between.

Such restraint is not easy. Without being aware of it, we are apt to resent our unaccustomed marginality and push ourselves to the fore, insisting we be noticed and acknowledged. We usually do this through mannerism or tone: stridency, sentimentality, cuteness. We do it, of course, in the name of God, supposing we are upholding the primacy of the one we represent. This is done with distressing regularity by pastors. But such posturing does not give glory to God; it only advertises clerical vanity. We are only hogging the show, and not very successfully, either. For no matter how resplendent we are in robes and "Reverends," we are no match for the persons or events that gave rise to the occasion to which we were asked to come and pray.

In Golden-Calf Country

But there is another reason for keeping to our position on the margins of ceremony and celebration. This is golden-calf country. Religious feeling runs high but in ways far removed from what was said on Sinai and done on Calvary. While everyone has a hunger for God, deep and insatiable, none of us has any great desire for him. What we really want is to be our own gods and to have whatever other gods that are around to help us in this work. This is as true for Christians as for non-Christians.

Our land lies east of Eden, and in this land, Self is sovereign. The catechetical instruction we grow up with has most of the questions couched in the first person: How can I make it? How can I maximize my potential? How can I develop my gifts? How can I overcome my handicaps? How can I cut my losses? How can I increase my longevity and live happily ever after, preferably all the way into eternity? Most of the answers to these questions include the suggestion that a little religion along the way wouldn't be a bad idea.

Every event that pulls us out of the ordinariness of our lives puts a little extra spin on these questions. Pastors, since we are usually present at the events and have a reputation of being knowledgeable in matters of religion, are expected to legitimize and encourage the religious dimensions in the aspirations. In our eagerness to please, and forgetful of the penchant for idolatry in the human heart, we too readily leave the unpretentious place of prayer and, with the freely offered emotional and religious jewelry the people bring, fashion a golden calf-god — Romantic Love, Beloved Memory, Innocent Life, Admirable Achievement — and proclaim a "feast to the Lord" (Ex. 32:5). Hardly knowing what we do, we meld the religious aspirations of the people and the religious dynamics of the occasion to try to satisfy one and all.

Calvin saw the human heart as a relentlessly efficient factory for producing idols. People commonly see the pastor as the quality-control engineer in the factory. The moment we accept the position, we defect from our vocation. People want things to work better; they want a life that is more interesting; they want help through a difficult time; they want meaning and significance in their ventures. They want God, in a way, but certainly not a "jealous God," not the "God and Father of our Lord Jesus Christ." Mostly they want to be their own god and stay in control, but have ancillary divine assistance for the hard parts.

There are a thousand ways of being religious without submitting to Christ's lordship, and people are practiced in most of them. They are trained from an early age to be discriminating consumers on their way to higher standards of living. It should be no great surprise when they expect pastors to help them do it. But it is a great apostasy when we go along. "And Moses said to Aaron, What did this people do to you that you have brought a great sin upon them?" (Ex. 32:21). Aaron's excuse is embarrassingly lame but more than matched by the justifications we make for abandoning prayer in our enthusiasm to make the most of the occasion.

Our Real Work

Our churches and communities assign us ceremonial duties on these occasions, which we must be careful to do well. There are right and wrong ways to act and speak, better and worse ways to prepare for and conduct these ceremonies and celebrations. No detail is insignificant: gesture conveys grace, tone of voice inculcates awe, demeanor defines atmosphere, preparation deepens wonder. We must be diligently skillful in all of this, and my colleagues in this book guide to competence in these matters.

But if there is no will to prayer in the pastor — a quietly stubborn and faithful centering in the action and presence of God — we will more than likely end up assisting, however inadvertently, in fashioning one more golden calf, of which the world has more than enough. What is absolutely critical is that we attend to God in these occasions: his Word, his Presence. We are there to say the Name, and by saying it guide lament into the depths where Christ descended into hell, not letting it digress into self-pity. We are there to say the Name, and by saying it direct celebration into praise of God, not letting it wallow in gossipy chatter.

Our real work in every occasion that requires a priestly presence is prayer. Whether anyone there knows or expects it, we arrive as persons of prayer. The margins are the best location for maintaining that intention. Our vocation is to be responsive to what God is saying at these great moments, and simply be there in that way as salt, as leaven.

Most of our prayer will be inaudible to those assembled. We are not praying to inspire them but to intercede for them. The action of God is intensified in these prayers and continued in the lives of the participants long after the occasion. The ceremonies are over in an hour or so; the prayers continue.

This is our real work: holding marriages and deaths, growing lives and lasting achievements before God in a continuing community of prayer.

T W O

CREATING A CLIMATE FOR LASTING MARRIAGES

The preparation I was giving couples once they had decided to be married seemed helpful as far as it went, but for an increasing number, it was simply too little, too late.

KEN WILSON

Laura was telling me about one of the best things God had ever brought into her life. His name was Jim: she loved to be with him; he was always on her mind; she felt more alive than she had ever felt before. Laura knew beyond a shadow of a doubt this was true love.

When I discovered Jim wasn't a Christian and I shared my concern about the handicap this would be to their unity, Laura wasn't fazed. It was as if I were criticizing his hair style. She was swept up in a wonderful feeling. I just didn't understand.

Laura married Jim, and sadly, now finds herself divorced.

John and Amy sat with nervous excitement in the chairs in my office. They had just announced their engagement and had come to me for "premarriage counseling." Their expectations, though unstated, were clear: I should warmly congratulate them, confer on a date for the wedding, give them a booklet on wedding plans, and offer pastoral perspective on what makes a marriage work.

There was only one problem: I wasn't sure this marriage

would work. Amy, I knew, was strong-willed, had a good deal of Christian training, and held high standards for Christian living. John, a fairly new Christian, tended toward moodiness. He was still working through some strong doubts.

I felt a responsibility to share my concerns and ask them to defer setting a date until these concerns were addressed. But I wondered whether this option was workable. They were, after all, deeply in love by this time. They had followed a typical American dating pattern that included a good deal of sexual contact short of actual intercourse. The emotional bond was set. Reason wasn't likely to break in at this point, and too much time might push the couple's remaining sexual restraint beyond the breaking point.

A Fresh Look

The discomfort of these and similar situations stirred me to take a fresh look at what we call marriage preparation. The preparation I was giving a couple once they had decided to be married seemed helpful as far as it went, but it was woefully inadequate for the increasing number of Lauras and Johns and Amys walking through the office door. It was simply too little, too late.

The other leaders of our fellowship and I began to consider: Rather than wring our hands over Laura and John and Amy, why not turn our attention to their younger brothers and sisters? Why not present an alternative to the young men and women who were just beginning to think of marriage, to help them choose a partner "in a way that is holy and honorable" (1 Thess. 4:3–5)?

Eventually we began to encourage an alternative approach to marriage preparation. And for all of the usual miscues in attempting a change this great, we have had unusual success in helping young people move into marriage and remain married. Since we began this approach, there have been many weddings — 160 in the last six years alone — and yet, among couples where both people were members of the fellowship and they remained in town (a high percentage of the marriages), I am not aware of a single divorce. There are some troubled marriages, but so far, these couples are staying together.

I am not suggesting we will never experience the pain of divorce; for one thing, these marriages have not yet gone the full distance. Nor am I suggesting our alternative approach to marriage preparation is solely, or even primarily, responsible. There are other factors: the comparatively high level of Christian commitment of our members and the fact that none of our leaders has been divorced, not to mention the grace of God underlying these. But the initial fruit encourages us that we have stumbled onto some important principles for creating a climate for lasting marriages.

Youth in our congregations face tough issues: How should I handle dating? What are the limits on sexual expression before marriage? How do I know when I'm ready to get married? How do I know if the person I'm attracted to is a good match?

They are getting radically different and opposing answers. It is hard to exaggerate the vast gulf between what our young people are being told by their peers and the media (which often seem to consider these questions obsolete), and what they are being told in our churches. All too often the church's advice gets left behind.

Lasting change begins when we understand the cultural tide we — and our young people — must swim against. Here, then, are our perceptions of the current cultural line on dating, sex, and courtship, and how we have responded to them.

Dating

I heard about a high school student who was asked by some of his buddies why he wasn't going to the prom.

"I don't know any girls who are worth the money," he replied, somewhat on the defensive.

They laughed and said, "But what about the sex? The sex is worth it."

Steeling his courage, he replied, "I'm not planning on having sex until I'm married."

His friends recommended a psychiatric evaluation.

While the bravado of young men often overstates reality, it is not uncommon for an invitation to the prom to connote an invitation to sex.

Statistics on the sexual activity of teenagers suggest this type of thinking is widespread. In a national Gallup survey in May 1981, 52 percent of the regular churchgoers ages 13–18 did not think premarital sex was wrong. In a survey of church-active Protestants in central Illinois, Steve Clapp found that 59 percent of the males 16–18 admitted having had intercourse, while 42 percent of the females admitted the same.

The role of dating in our society has changed over the past thirty years. Dating has become detached from the process of looking for a marriage partner; it is no longer primarily a courtship activity but a recreational activity. Anyone who thinks recreational dating doesn't encourage sexual activity has lost his appreciation for the obvious. But there are other problems.

We noticed one in our early work with university students. The preoccupation with romantic relationships was threatening to turn the group into something of a soap opera. As young people paired up and split up, relationships were strained and jealousies created. The less-attractive and less-popular students often felt isolated, left out, and resentful. The whole process made young people more self-conscious: "Am I attractive?" "Why isn't anyone asking me out?"

A third and related problem: Dating was not helping train them for married life. The strong focus on one-on-one relationships with someone of the opposite sex short-circuited kids from building a wider base of strong relationships. Relying on one person for most of one's social and emotional needs began a pattern that often burdened the marriage relationship later.

I've found young people are not as resistant to acknowledging these pitfalls as one might expect. They admit the many pressures, frustrations, and temptations of the typical dating scene. Consequently, many of them have taken seriously our counsel: Until you are ready to begin seeking a spouse, don't date. Look for opportunities to be with members of the opposite sex in group situations.

Of course, this means we have to work to do two things: teach young people about Christian relationships, beginning early, and provide them with positive group social opportunities.

Our fellowship operates a Christian school for fourth through ninth grades, and we begin there. We talk openly about an alternative approach to dating. We discourage the flirtation and pairing off so common in junior high schools.

With high school students, we work to build an environment that supports the students who have decided to forgo romantic relationships until they are ready for marriage. This isn't easy, but through a variety of means — retreats, some small groups, even large-group activities — young people can share their struggles and get support for taking a Christian stand.

Our fellowship has long had an extensive outreach to university students, and we've found them the most receptive of all. High school young people, while they are the least equipped to handle dating, are the most pressured into it. By college, some of the intense peer pressure can lessen. We sponsor many group events for university students. Better still, we've discovered, are group service projects. When young men and women work together in Bible studies for new believers, they get to know each other without the self-consciousness of dating.

Sex in Courtship

Jim was involved in a courtship process — dating a young woman and trying to decide whether they ought to get married. As we talked about it, Jim wondered about my view on the role of sex in courtship. I told him. His face told me he considered me reactionary and prudish. He asked, "But how are we going to know whether we are sexually compatible?"

The question is not moot: What is the place of sexual activity in the courtship process?

Our youth may not agree that sexual intercourse before marriage is wrong. (According to the Clapp study, 48 percent of the Protestant church-active boys and girls between 13 and 15 years of age said sexual intercourse was OK as long as the couple were in love, even if unmarried.) But even among those who hold strongly that sex before marriage is wrong, many would draw a sharp distinction between sexual inter-course and the range of sexual interaction that stops short of intercourse.

Here I must disagree. My experience with young people convinces me the wisest, most biblically sound, and healthiest answer is simply: sexual activity *of any kind* is best reserved for marriage. The sexual encounter is by nature progressive: one thing is designed to lead to another. We are psychologically and biologically designed to experience a compelling sense of momentum that begins with sexually significant touch and light kissing, moves to heavy kissing and petting, and ends with intercourse.

Young people, by the way, understand this. If I'm counsel-ing a young man in this area and sense resistance, I may ask him to consider his own experience. Has he ever been in-volved in prolonged kissing and noticed the onset of an erec-tion? From a creation perspective, what purpose would God have in mind for linking an erection with such activity? I know that's direct, even blunt, but I've found it helps young people accept my case for stricter standards, and often they thank me for being straightforward.

But for some reason we have a reluctance to reach the obvious conclusion. We shy away from confidently urging couples to avoid the whole range of sexual activity that pre-cedes intercourse. But what good is gained by tacitly approv-ing preliminary sexual contact when it so powerfully and easily leads further?

This reasoning runs contrary to the cultural currents of our society. Teaching helps, but I've found personal discussions with the people currently facing the issues to be most effective. Often I'll share the experience of others.

When Jim came to me, for example, I told him about a married couple I know that had fooled around more than they had intended to before they got married. They both felt disappointed in themselves and began their sexual relationship in marriage feeling vaguely guilty. The wife had lost a measure of trust in her husband's ability to control his sexual desire, and it made it more difficult for her to respond to him sexually. Now they wish they had drawn a clearer line and observed it.

I told him of a woman I'd talked with who had spent a few months dating a young man. As time went on, the two of them expressed more and more physical affection, up to and including a little petting. All this had a profound effect on the woman; she developed a strong emotional bond with the man. The physical affection didn't seem to have nearly the same effect on him. When he decided they were probably not a good match, it was difficult for him to end the relationship, but it devastated her. Something had begun to form in her that was now being torn.

And since the best illustrations are positive, I tell counselees about several young couples I know who were married with no more than hand holding, walking arm in arm, and an occasional good-night kiss — and that only after they were engaged. Their sexual adjustment in marriage is better than that of many couples I know who were sexually active before marriage.

Selecting a Mate

Many young people have a romantic expectation of meeting someone who is erotically attractive and elicits a mysterious sense of compatibility. "Falling in love" hits like a powerful religious experience and is taken to be the voice of God: "This is the one for you." Christian young people are sitting ducks for this deception.

They need compelling instruction that identifies Christian love as service love, founded on a decision, drawing from the emotions but not grounded in them. They also need wise criteria for selecting a spouse. We suggest they consider questions like the following:

— What kind of life is God calling you to live? What kind of spouse would support that?

— What kind of person would likely make a good father or mother for your children?

— What personality traits would put additional stress on your personal weaknesses?

— What are the important qualities in a spouse "for the long haul"? How do attractive appearance and an urbane sense of humor rate over time with a trait like faithfulness?

We realize we're asking people to consider selecting a mate (and the dating process that precedes it) from a perspective entirely different from what they may be used to. So we try to provide instruction not only to young people but also to parents and the body at large so they can support them.

When people join our community, they take an extensive course in the basics of the Christian faith. During part of the course, we pay special attention to relationships and a Christian approach to sexuality, dating, marriage, and commitment. This helps our members have a common perspective on these matters.

Some parents are less sure about our counsel on dating than their kids. They remember their own dating from thirty years ago, which may have been relatively tame, and aren't aware of the increased pressure toward sexual activity today. Or they want their kids to be accepted and fear if they don't date extensively, they won't be. So we address these issues in regular courses on family life and monthly forums for parents and teachers. Naturally these sessions cover a variety of topics — right now, the special demands of raising pre-schoolers — but encouraging teenagers to have a healthy approach to sexuality is a key concern.

Small Beginnings

The challenge to build a climate for lasting marriages can seem overwhelming, but there are small beginnings that are well within reach. Preaching in this area helps. So does an occasional class for junior high and senior high students.

But the best strategy in many situations may be to begin with a few committed people. This became clear to me one day when Rick came to see me. Rick had made a weak commitment to Christ when he was a child. Now as a university student he had come to a deeper conversion and was serious about his faith. He had recently broken up with his girlfriend because he knew their relationship wasn't pleasing to God.

Rick told me, "I want to approach every area of my life as a disciple. I want my future relationships with women to be in the Lord." He wanted to know how a Christian should approach dating and preparation for marriage.

Every young person in our congregations is not going to have the commitment of Rick. We soon saw, however, that special pastoral attention to the most highly motivated young men and women is time well spent. Those who have successfully adopted the approach of "taking a wife in honor" become advocates and tutors of an alternative approach to younger members.

As Zechariah prophesied, "Do not despise the day of small beginnings" (Zech. 4:10). Even if we begin to work with only a few adventurous volunteers — perhaps even one — we can be confident that small seeds bearing the character of the kingdom will flourish.

THREE

SHOULD WE MARRY THE UNCHURCHED?

For the first time in their lives, they want something from the church, really want *something.*

Douglas G. Scott

The pattern is familiar: A couple calls the church office to say they are planning to be married and want to arrange a wedding in the church. They are not members of this church (or perhaps they were members years ago but haven't been to church since confirmation). They may not even be members of the denomination, but they "knew someone who was married at St. Swithin's two years ago."

How should we respond? What are the pastoral possibilities inherent in these situations?

Many clergy dismiss such calls immediately, explaining that they perform services only for members of their own congregation. Others may see some of the couples and make a decision to perform the ceremony on the basis of the couple's rudimentary understanding of the Christian faith. Still others act as ecclesiastical marriage brokers, performing the ceremony for any and all who ask, usually beefing up their discretionary fund in the process.

After struggling with these questions for some time, I have devised an approach, based on a number of theological suppositions, that seems to work well.

Why Are They Here?

My primary assumption about all the individuals who call is that *they have been prompted to call by the Holy Spirit.* To be sure, they are probably unaware of this prompting, but in each of these situations, I assume that God is giving me an opportunity to do some serious examination with the couple about the nature and quality of Christian marriage.

The couple may have their own reasons for calling the church, and each of them is woefully familiar to every minister:

"Your church is so pretty."

"Your church is close to our reception hall."

"My second cousin was married here by the minister who was here before you."

Their initial reason for calling is unimportant. The Holy Spirit has prompted them to call your church, even if yours is the fourth or fifth on a list of possible places. You have been presented with an unparalleled opportunity to reach out with Christ's love to two people who may have never before experienced it in all its fullness. I don't dismiss such opportunities quickly.

My second assumption when the unchurched call is that *this may be the first time they have ever turned to the church for help.* If they are a young couple, both sets of parents are probably still living, and there is a good chance, given increasing rates of longevity, that the grandparents are living as well. Consequently, this couple may never have had an opportunity or the need to turn to the church in time of crisis. While they may have attended Sunday school in childhood, their most recent experience of church was probably a Christmas Eve service a number of years ago. For the first time in their lives, they want something from the church, really *want* something.

Our initial response to their call will determine whether they see the church as cold and unresponsive, or open and responsive to those outside as well as inside its fellowship.

My third assumption is that *there are some shreds of spiritual awareness which prompt them to seek marriage in the church.* To be sure, a certain percentage of the couples who call want a church wedding only because "it's traditional," or because their parents insist. However, we must also recognize that for others, there are certain events in their lives that they see as "religious moments." While they may want to confine their experience of God to controlled and predictable encounters, there are moments when they feel God should be included.

My fourth assumption (especially if they have no prior connection with the parish I serve) is that *there may have been a problem with a previous church affiliation.* Perhaps one of them is divorced and is not permitted to remarry in his or her own denomination, or perhaps one was treated harshly by a former pastor. Perhaps they themselves were difficult and alienated themselves from the life of their initial church home and have not since been affiliated with a community of faith. In any event, they may well be spiritually homeless, and they have turned to your church. They may not be looking for a church home, but they are asking to use the house.

On the basis of these assumptions, I have determined to consent to at least meet with each couple that calls inquiring about marriage.

The Initial Telephone Call

I attempt to do some initial screening on the telephone, and I include a very clear explanation of what can be expected from me. I determine where both parties live, their ages, and previous religious affiliation, if any. I ask if there were previous marriages, and if so, how long the divorce decree has been final, and where it was granted. Is at least one of the parties baptized? Have they sought to be married by another member of the clergy and been refused?

I explain to the caller that I will be glad to see the couple but that my consenting to see them does not mean I will guarantee to marry them. I insist that the interview be with both bride and groom, and that no other family members be present or accompany them. I explain that the purpose of the interview will be to determine whether we can speak seriously about being married in the church, and that at the conclusion of the interview, I may consent to marry them, but in all probability, no decision will be reached for some weeks. I then set a mutually convenient time when the couple can meet with me in the office, explaining that they should expect to be with me for at least an hour.

One postscript: I do not make appointments on the basis of a mother's telephone request. When a mother calls, I simply explain that I will be glad to discuss the possibility when her daughter or son calls, but that the couple must take the responsibility themselves for arranging the interview.

The Initial Interview

The attitude of most couples with no parish affiliation who come for an initial premarital interview falls usually into one of two categories—apprehensive or arrogant. They are either nervous, not knowing what to expect, or they are openly disdainful of this situation, which they consider a necessary evil. In any event, they are rarely comfortable. While some clergy might not try to dispel this feeling, thus retaining an edge or advantage, I try to make the couple as comfortable as possible, remembering that they will probably judge this "church business" by their impressions of who I am and how I respond to their presence.

After exchanging pleasantries, I turn immediately to the form that catalogs all necessary information required by the state and my denomination. I do this simply in question-and-answer form, and include questions of the date they had in mind, the names of their intended witnesses, and their permanent address after marriage. The last piece of information allows me to contact the church of my denomination closest to them for the purpose of referral, should they be moving some distance from this parish.

I do not ask why they want to be married. After interviewing hundreds of couples, I have never found one that gives me an answer other than "Because we love each other." Obviously, the age of the couple may make it necessary to determine whether this, in fact, is intended as a marriage or as an escape from a difficult family or personal situation. However, if they are both of reasonable age, and there are no legal or ecclesiastical impediments, I turn immediately to the meat of the interview.

My initial presentation usually runs like this:

"Let me say at the outset that I am not here to sit in judgment on you. You have decided that you want to marry each other, and since there are no legal impediments that I can determine, you have every right to do so. You have decided to marry, and I am not going to try to change your mind. Our purpose today is simply to determine whether or not this marriage should begin in the church.

"Now the state and the church view marriage very differently. In the eyes of the state, marriage is little more than a contractual agreement — the two of you agree, by contract, to do certain things for each other, and make promises about how you will conduct your life together. The contract is witnessed by two individuals of legal age. At any point in the contract, you may seek to have that contract dissolved through the process we call divorce. That is how the state views marriage, and this can be performed by a judge or a mayor.

"The church's view of marriage, however, is very different. So let me begin by asking: What do you really want? Do you simply want to be married, or do you want to commit yourselves to the unique responsibilities of Christian marriage?"

This presentation is usually followed by a silence of considerable length as the couple look at me with a blank stare. I have on occasion had a couple respond that they simply want to be married. At that point I reply, "I'm sorry, I don't perform weddings — I preside at the services of the church. If I had known that was all you wanted, I could have saved you the trip here. Thank you for coming." On those occasions, the couple, flustered by the swiftness of the dismissal, invariably back down and begin to explain what they meant by their prompt response. The door remains open.

More often than not, however, the couple, after sitting in silence for some time, ask what I mean. The opportunity for a teaching dialogue between clergy and couple has been presented. I usually proceed in a question-and-answer format designed to get the couple talking about the nature and depth of their personal spiritual development and the impact of that development on their common life. Some of the questions might take the following forms:

How would you describe your relationship with God? What role does God play in your daily life?

What does God expect of a couple who begin their married life in the church? Have you discussed your mutual responsibilities as a Christian couple?

How would you say Christian marriage differs from other marriages?

Do you worship together? Do you feel comfortable with the idea of praying together? Why or why not?

To be sure, most unchurched couples take the attitude "I try to live a good life and be nice to people," but this avoidance of the issue must be pointed out. I make a clear distinction between being a Christian and being "nice" (or altruistic or philanthropic or compassionate). What I seek is a clear definition of their concept of the action of God in their lives, and their response to that action. There are some couples who don't seem to get the point, and a potential device for clarifying the issue might be: "Your relationship as a couple has a number of different dimensions — a social dimension (you date, share common activities and friends), an emotional dimension (you have feelings toward and about each other that satisfy each other's emotional needs), a financial dimension (you have made decisions about your common property, how your money will be handled, who will work, and at what job), a physical dimension (the sexual expression of your emotions), and a spiritual dimension. How do you see yourselves as spiritual persons, and how do you relate on a spiritual level with each other, and with God?"

Following this exploration, the couple has usually come up with one of two answers — either they realize there is a neglected aspect of their relationship and are anxious to develop that aspect, or they state that their commitment to the Christian faith is marginal at best and that they have no intention of associating with a church following the marriage ceremony. If the former situation arises, I have an opportunity to provide direction about the development of the Christian faith in this embryonic stage. If the latter presents itself, I usually use the following approach:

"I am not a baseball fan. Understand, I believe in baseball — that is, I believe baseball exists and that there are many people whose happiness depends, in part, on the fortunes of a particular team. They go to each of the home games, wear team jackets, and put team decals on their cars. I can believe all of those things, but I am not a fan. I don't enjoy going to baseball games, and whether the Mets win or lose is of no importance to me at all. It would be strange, therefore, if I wanted to have my wedding in Shea Stadium! You see, when you are married in the church, you ask for the blessing, approval, and support of God's family as you begin your married life, because God's family is important to you. During a church wedding, you make promises to each other, and to God, about your life together and your life as members of God's family."

At that point, I discuss the specific expectations of Christian marriage and the commitments made by the couple toward the church in that ceremony. Then, "Since you have made it clear that you have no commitment to the church, do you feel comfortable making solemn promises about your future involvement with the church?"

The device is obvious. Rather than making the decision for them, you present them with the teaching of the church and ask them to make the decision. Most couples have a sense of integrity and say they weren't aware that this was what happened in the context of the ceremony. Frequently, they say they would rather be married in a civil ceremony than to make promises they don't intend to keep. Occasionally, they say they still want to be married in the church, and at that point, you can justifiably state some expectations:

"You say you want to go ahead and make these promises to each other and to God. Each of you is willing to make these commitments to each other because you have seen some evidence that those promises are already being fulfilled. If you are serious about making these promises to God, why don't you start fulfilling them now, and see how you feel about making a long-term commitment later. That is, let's say that you begin attending church and working at your Christian relationship, and forgo making a decision about marriage in the church until you have had an opportunity to see how it 'feels.' In two months, after you have attended church together for a while, let's get together again and talk about the next step — making a long-term commitment to establishing a Christian relationship."

At that point, some couples say they have no intention of adhering to those expectations. In that event, they have made the decision: they do not wish to be married in the church if it entails attendance and support. I then thank them for their time and wish them well in their life together. They may, on the other hand, agree to those conditions, at which point I have provided the couple with an opportunity for involvement with the community of faith.

Every attempt should be made to integrate the couple into the life of the congregation as soon as possible. Usually, their involvement leads to commitment.

The Second Interview

The content of the second interview is determined by the couple's response to the conditions established at the first one. If they have expressed a desire to explore the spiritual aspect of their relationship and have agreed to a "trial period" of church involvement, we then discuss how they feel about their involvement thus far.

On occasion, couples have determined that church life is not for them, and they decide to forgo a church wedding in favor of a civil ceremony. More often than not, however, they have, through the movement of the Holy Spirit, found the richness inherent in Christian living and want to pursue their faith even further. A small percentage of couples agree to a period of church involvement but fail to fulfill that agreement. If that is the case, I express my confusion, saying, "You are ready to make lifelong promises to your partner because he or she is already, in a partial way, fulfilling those promises. If you didn't see those promises being fulfilled, you would be skeptical about them being kept after the marriage ceremony. You have not demonstrated to me that you are ready to fulfill the promises you would be asked to make in a church wedding. Let me ask you again. Are you ready to commit yourselves to a Christian marriage?"

I have rarely had to refuse a couple. Usually they decide on their own either to commit themselves to the church or to seek a civil ceremony. From their response to the situations presented them, I tell the couple, in effect, that they have already made the decision about whether or not they really want to be married in the church, and that I agree (or disagree) with their decision. We then can plan the wedding itself, including a time for in-depth marital counseling.

The Counseling Phase

A significant portion of the premarital counseling process involves directing the couple toward full involvement in the life of the congregation. Pastors of other denominations might use a different approach, but I invariably urge the couple to attend adult inquirer classes that lead to confirmation. If they are lapsed members of my denomination, I suggest that they request to be transferred from their home parish.

But more important, I emphasize not only technical membership in the church but active involvement as well. Themes centering on stewardship of their time, talent, and treasure fit

naturally into the premarital program, and I see that they a
directed toward programs or service groups within the co
gregation that would further heighten their interest a
participation. In planning any fellowship or social function
make sure the couple receives a personal invitation, eithe
handwritten note or a telephone call, from another membei
the congregation, thus making them feel more a part of t
parish family. The congregation I serve responds warmly
the presence of newcomers. The couple quickly feels at hom

By using an approach that places the onus of the decisi
on the couple rather than the minister, I feel I fulfill a numl
of desirable goals. This approach provides an attitude
openness and caring; offers an opportunity for growth, teac
ing, and commitment; and most of all, allows the couple
have equity in the nature of their commitment to each oth
and to God. They make the decisions and, having made the
are far more likely to fulfill the obligations inherent in Chi
tian marriage.

FOUR

PREMARITAL PASTORING

I find couples open to building the best marriage they possibly can; my aim is to coach them toward that goal.

BRUCE ROWLISON

A psychologist once said to me bluntly, "Don't send me any more premarriage counseling. The couples aren't in crisis. They don't want to work on their relationship. They just want to get married. They are less in love than they are in heat. You keep them, Pastor."

I don't agree with his conclusion, but that conversation forced me to question my premarital ministry to couples.

Gradually I began to see myself as more of a coach than a counselor. A coach discovers and points out skills already there, then tries to motivate people to increase those skills and gain new ones. In premarital counseling, I find couples *open* to building the best marriage they possibly can; my aim is to coach them toward that goal.

Still, the couple's affection for each other is so intense it does periodically block the rational. They seem to float above my office couch, rather than sit comfortably on it. But in spite of all their anxiety and impatience, meaningful things happen in our times together.

Establishing a Relationship

I begin by building a friendship. I'm convinced learning increases as trust and respect are established. Plus, my God is personal. He knows me by name. So, I spend time getting acquainted.

Right at the beginning I tell them, "In order to personalize your wedding, I need to get acquainted with you both. Hopefully, the information we share will build our friendship, and I expect our relationship to continue beyond the wedding."

I begin with positive, easy questions: How did you meet? What have been some of the most enjoyable times you've had together? How did you come to the conclusion that this is the one you want to marry?

I'm beginning to collect information on their relationship skills, attitude toward marriage, and openness to my input. The quality of this time often determines the effectiveness of our sessions. I acknowledge and honor their right to pass over a subject they are uncomfortable discussing with me at this stage. (Who wants to be lied to anyway?) I tell them I consider it a privilege to share in this pivotal point in their journey, the beginning of their married life.

After establishing rapport, I begin to ask the more difficult questions, such as, "Which of you felt the most discomfort in coming to see me, and why?" I ask them to describe their visits with each other's families, because those are often the most stressful times in courtship.

Seeing Eye to Eye

I'm now ready to move toward some agreement for the rest of our time together. My transition question is, "Before we go any further, I need to check if you have some expectations of our time together. What are your special interests or needs, so I'm sure to budget time for them?" I listen as much for what they don't expect as for their expectations.

Then I often give a sixty-second synopsis of who I am, what I have been through in life, what skills I have that might be helpful to them, and where I'm weak: "I'm not a psychologist. I'm a pastor. A lot of my work has to do with marriage. I have skills in listening and clarifying. I don't try to change people's personalities. So relax. I'm not good in money management, but we have a banker and two realtors in the church who will help you free of charge. Here are some options for us to work on in our times together. You pick three or four, and I'll pick three or four, and we'll have a good time together."

Among my list of options:
— misconceptions of love and marriage
— games that can increase friendship
— practical issues in marriage (money, sex and affection, role expectations, values, religious faith, power and freedom, communication, and nurture)
— romantic love
— Christian marriage.

I believe in offering choices because it shifts responsibility to them. In my early years, I left the office exhausted while the couple departed bored. They had watched me do marvelous things for ninety minutes: lecture on sexuality, supply money management insights taken from a speech by a well-known economist, administer probing quizzes and diagnose the quality of their relationship. But I've changed my style to become the coach who helps *them* do the work.

I don't even administer psychological tests and inventories any more. I am not against testing. I simply find that such instruments tend to raise the couple's anxiety level, and one of my goals is to reduce any sense of threat so they can deal with their actual needs and worries.

Misconceptions

One "test" I do give is called "Misconceptions of Love and Marriage." I make a game out of it; I laugh and overdramatize it. I tell them I won't give them the answers unless they tie me to the chair and threaten my life, because the purpose is to stimulate conversation, not right or wrong answers. In this test they are supposed to mark various statements as true or false:
— Loneliness will be cured by marriage.

— Crying is something to be avoided in marriage.

— Getting angry is better than being critical.

The list contains twenty-five such statements.[1]

Amazing things happen in these moments. They laugh. They disagree openly. They get nervous. They show frustration. They reveal expectations. Sometimes they begin to ask for information. But my goal is for *them* to do the talking. I stimulate their conversation. As a pastor trained to correct wrong thinking, I have to bite my tongue here. Later I will teach them, but now, through their conversation, I get an immediate feel for how naive or informed they are.

If I'm working with a couple struggling to articulate feelings, or with a couple where one person dominates the conversation and the other grunts or nods, I shift our direction and suggest we play another game. I have some toys that represent real-life things, such as Monopoly money, a plastic telephone, a baby doll. They reach into the bag, pull something out, and state what the item means to them or how they feel about it. One man took out the telephone, threw it across the room, and exclaimed, "I hate the thing. It's always interrupting my time with people." The nonverbal communication becomes more animated as well — the way they handle each object, facial responses, glances, and gestures. I've been amazed at how these simple toys help couples relax and begin to talk more openly.

Practical Issues

I spend the bulk of my time on "practical issues in love and marriage" to prepare couples for the early adjustment stages of marriage. I want them aware of some of the complexities, conflicts, and struggles. I ask each person to pick a section of this topic, and I begin with the one the least-verbal partner selected.

I try to fill these moments with humor and anecdotes, employing hypothetical situations to watch for their responses. I might say, "The basic approach to money in my family, growing up, was to save. We never had much, but out of our meager resources we were disciplined to save something. The problem was, we never knew what we were saving for. The terms 'rainy day' and 'emergency' were used frequently but never defined. We were glad we weren't like neighbors across the street who 'always fought about how they would invest.' Does this ring any bells with you?"

Another goal of mine is to model openness on topics that have been taboo previously, such as sex, money, or anger.

If they respond strongly to any one point, I concentrate on that area. I draw them out, ask if they would like more information, listen actively, give feedback, point out resources in the church family to help them.

• *Affection and sexuality.* I spend a lot of time on affection and sexuality. I start by sharing a statement by David Hubbard that I have found to be true: "Remember, men and women, because of Genesis 3 and the sin in the Garden of Eden, everyone you meet will be confused sexually and have a problem with idolatry." I point out I fall into that category, as do family members, doctors, parents, and friends. We all struggle to find accurate sexual information. So, where do you find information on sexuality? What is sexual love? What will you do if one of you is more highly sexed than the other? I ask lots of questions and hold back information until I perceive eagerness or receptivity on their part.

I find the affection and caring/intimacy side of sexuality is often neglected and misunderstood. An area of tension even among Christians (perhaps especially among Christians) is the issue of what is one person's right to know about the other's sexual past. I don't try to press my ideas on them. My greatest concern is that they agree about how much candor they can expect from each other.

Another factor increasingly affecting sexuality today is traumatic sexual experiences such as rape or incest. Gently raising that issue and reassuring them that professional help is available may be my greatest contribution to their sexual compatibility. I hope to lead them into a deeper level of communication than they have previously experienced.

A Lutheran friend acts as a priest at this point in his coaching. He receives confession, pronounces absolution, and sets them free for a new direction in life. Sometimes he anoints with oil. Often he cries with them. He is continually amazed at the visible change this effects in couples.

If the couple is new to the church, I ask them to articulate their formative church's views on marital roles. Role expectations — the meaning of headship and submissiveness, the need for increased emotional support, the level of financial support expected — are being debated fiercely in the Christian community today. I find this a major area where modern marriages are exploding. Who determines the roles? How well are they articulated? What happens if roles change with the coming of children or sickness? I try to be pointedly practical.

● *Values.* To break the question-answer pattern, I treat the values area more creatively. "Draw your family crest," I tell them, "selecting symbols that represent what was important to you growing up." In another exercise, I give them colored cards and ask them to write their values on them, red for nonnegotiable values, yellow for important but modifiable ones, and green for flexible ones. The values deal with such issues as types of occupation, whether and when to have children, and family life.

"I must have passion in marriage," one woman said, leaning forward with her jaw firm.

"What constitutes passion for you, and what are some things that arouse it and things that kill it?" I responded. "Do you know where that need comes from and why it is so intense?"

When she answered, I asked her fiancé what he heard her say. I then asked, "Are you both willing to commit money, time, and energy to that value?" These understandings or misunderstandings prove crucial to a marriage.

● *Religious faith.* If they don't select the religious faith section, I do. I spin life stories of how different religious journeys develop or clash. I encourage them to share their faith adventure with me. This is an area where couples are often vague and mystical. They tend to romanticize. So I press for concreteness: "How often do you expect to go to church?" "Tell me about the last time your fiancée said, 'I'm sorry. I was wrong. Will you forgive me?'"

• *Power and freedom.* This is the area in which I have made the most misjudgments. I send couples to a Christian counselor, saying, "The man is a tyrant." Then I'll sit in on a session with the couple and the therapist, and he'll say, "She is in total control. Did you see the way he jumped when she coughed? Did you see him stop talking when she frowned at him?"

I'm not hesitant to admit inadequacy in any section where I'm weak. I'll give them names of Christian counselors as resources. I can't do all things for them, and it is wise to tell them that.

• *Communication.* This is one area in which I try to secure a promise from them. I say, "You promise God in the wedding service that you will love each other. To preserve communication, will you promise each other you will have a weekly business meeting to check out your calendar and emotional well-being? And will you commit to two mini-honeymoons yearly, even if they are only overnight?"

• *Nurture.* Mutual nurture is my special emphasis. I am amazed at how few people have articulated how they want to be nurtured (even those married ten and twenty years). We tend to nurture a spouse in the way *we* want to be nurtured. But our approach to nurturing can aggravate the spouse we intend to lovingly support. The wife, who might be nurtured by exercise, may be always buying jogging suits, stationary bicycles, tennis shoes, and racketball equipment for her spouse, who hates athletics and loves his night at home by the fire with a good book. My aim is for couples to respect each other's nurture needs, even if they don't understand them.

I know I can't resolve all these practical issues for a couple, but I can raise their awareness of them. I can open the issues and tell them help is available. Later, if conflicts increase, I hope they won't be paralyzed and do nothing until the problem reaches a catastrophic level.

I give homework assignments to check a couple's motivational level. Outside assignments also help information move from their heads to the gut. I assign couples the task of looking up some Bible passages that teach about marriage and writing one sentence about each passage. I intend this launching into the Scriptures in a general way to impress them with the reality that God designed marriage for specific reasons and has exciting things to say about how marriage works best. We'll talk later about the passages. One of my goals is for them to experience God's love and presence in their relationship.

The Meaning of Christian Marriage

I shift next to the area of contract and covenant in marriage. I explain how psychologists today argue that every marriage has a contract, perhaps implied if not written out or discussed, and usually both parties perceive the contract differently. I take them through an actual contract of a couple who are friends of mine. Again, I make a game of it, asking them where they think the marriage almost blew apart.

In my experience, this is the most potentially explosive portion of our time together. "I have the right of access to your schedule," one woman fumed as she and her fiancé formed their contract in front of me.

"No way!" he shouted back. "I go where I want to go and do what I want to do just like during our engagement."

"Unacceptable," she replied. "That is not a marriage." They argued a few more minutes and then jumped up and left my office never to return — and never to marry. I often reflect on how important it was for them to discover that polarization before they made their big step.

I don't want to leave any couple at the contract stage. The sacred bond of covenant transcends the legal ties of marriage. So we discuss at length God's commitment to their union and how it symbolizes to a non-Christian world the commitment of God to his people.

Agreeing on the Service

I end my time with a couple by going through the wedding service line by line. I have gathered copies of five different vows, from high church to contemporary. I ask them to select the ones that best express their theology, taste, and feelings. Rarely has a couple said, "No, you choose one, Pastor."

From the central aspect of the vows, I move backward in the wedding service to explain the questions of intent, the meaning of the Scripture readings and prayers. Then I sit back and watch them do all the work of deciding what they want included in their service, and in what form. Through their interactions I can see how they make decisions.

When they are finished, *they* have designed their wedding service — within the limits I have set. Couples find it exhilarating. I ask my secretary to type the service, and we deliver several copies to them.

Like any pastor, I have room to improve my premarital ministry to couples. One area I am currently studying is how to better relate couples to the church's ongoing program of marriage enrichment. But my ministry is working. By the time we reach the wedding event:

— We have built a warm and trusting relationship.

— I have involved them in the process by giving them choices.

— They have articulated their expectations.

— We have studied practical issues, and I have conveyed critical information in important areas.

— They have practiced and strengthened their communication skills.

— I have modeled and they have experienced openness on subjects that might have been taboo previously.

— We have shared the presence of Christ together.

— Study of Scripture and the meaning of covenant has helped them understand the difference between getting married and holy matrimony.

— They have begun to articulate the rules of their relationship.

— Perhaps there has been confession, with forgiveness pronounced and experienced.

— They are aware of where to turn for help in the years ahead.

— The wedding service will express their unique relationship.

Building the best possible marriages remains a lofty goal, but for the health of the home and the church, it is a worthwhile pursuit. And I would find premarital conversations worthwhile if only the first goal were achieved — a warm and trusting relationship established between me and the couple. Just as marriage gives couples a secure environment in which to grow and reach out, the relationship I've begun with a couple offers a secure step to a deeper relationship with the church and her Bridegroom.

---

1. The complete list is available in *Let's Talk about Your Wedding & Marriage* by Bruce Rowlison and George Hinn, available through Green Leaf Press, P. O. Box 6880, Alhambra, California 91802.

FIVE

THE REHEARSAL AND CEREMONY

As pastors we have the best seat in the house; we witness pointblank the tender exchange of a loving couple's commitment before God, their family, and friends.

R. KENT HUGHES

Almost everyone has a "wedding story" to tell, and it's usually slapstick. From the twenty years I have performed weddings, I have my share.

I've seen grooms so wobbly-kneed they had to be propped in a chair to finish the ceremony.

On other occasions, despite my traditional caveat to the wedding party not to lock their legs lest circulation be cut off and someone pass out, that warning seems only to function as a "sure word of prophecy." At one of those times, a garden wedding, the groom's brother crashed into the ivy during the prayer and did not wake up until after the kiss. The next week I dramatically warned another wedding party, using my fresh illustration. The result? The bride's brother passed out, also during the prayer, and actually bounced on the slate floor, again missing the nuptial salute! The best-laid plans . . .

Another time the groomsmen and ushers were shorted a couple of bow ties by their tuxedo service, which created a comical Laurel-and-Hardy foyer as they frantically exchanged ties as their duties came up.

Weddings, because they are idealized and romanticized, provide ample occasion for such "disasters," which invariably become fond memories as the years pass. "Remember when Uncle Joe hit the ivy?" "Yeah, it was great!"

Yet for the most part, weddings are wonderfully uneventful, and the pastor's participation a pleasant remembrance. As pastors we have the best seat in the house; we witness pointblank the tender exchange of a loving couple's commitment before God, their family, and friends. We see the flushed cheeks, moist eyes, trembling hands, and the nuanced gestures of this most sacred time. It is an immense privilege.

What are the important principles in planning and carrying out this privilege? How do we minimize the follies and maximize the sacredness? The key is to remember — throughout the planning, rehearsal, and the ceremony itself — that the Christian wedding is a *worship* celebration. As we will see, this has several practical implications.

The Planning Session

Early in the preparation stage, usually about four months before the wedding, I invite the couple to my office to plan the ceremony, urging that both attend, if possible. I normally schedule thirty and no more than forty-five minutes for this time.

With coffee in hand and after we have visited a few minutes and prayed, I briefly outline the theology of Christian marriage. I emphasize that a wedding ceremony is a time of worship, of reverence, because in Christian marriage the man and woman commit themselves to God as well as to each other (Rom. 12:1). I point out that while their human relationship will be showcased in the ceremony, it is not to be a show, for worship cannot be so.

Personally, I'm glad we seem to have passed the period when each wedding had to be a self-conscious production, with colored tuxes, bride and groom singing to each other, and lots of pressure on everyone to perform for the crowd. Lance Morrow, in a 1983 *Time* essay titled "The Hazards of Homemade Vows," warns against making the ceremony a display case for unbridled creativity:

"Some couples remain tempted by the opportunity a wedding offers for self-expression. It is a temptation that should be resisted. . . . If the bride and groom have intimacies to whisper, there are private places for that. A wedding is public business. That is the point of it. The couple are not merely marrying one another. They are, at least in part, submitting themselves to the larger logics of life, to the survival of the community, to life itself. . . . At the moment of their binding, they should subsume their egos into that larger business within which their small lyricisms become tinny and exhibitionistic."

Also, while it is nice to have the vows memorized, generally I discourage couples who want to recite them from memory during the ceremony. The stress of the wedding day is enough without this added pressure. I want the couple to relax, to enjoy the event, to *worship* as effectively as possible.

So I make sure the couple understands these implications of planning the ceremony as a worship service.

But at the same time, I emphasize that worship does not mean the ceremony has to be somber. We're celebrating a wedding, not a funeral. I remind them that Christ saw weddings as occasions of great joy. In fact he performed his first miracle at a tiny wedding in Cana, changing the water to wine, a symbol of joy. Thus the wedding is worshipful and joyful celebration — and that is what I hope to help them achieve. Here, I always stress how honored I am to participate in such an event.

Next I give them a Wedding Ceremony Planning Sheet (see end of chapter), which outlines a typical ceremony. I explain this is simply a suggested outline — the order is negotiable, as are the contents. If there are other elements they prefer, they will probably be okay, if appropriate for worship.

The planning sheet, I've found, has a calming effect on the couple. The typical bride and groom are intimidated by the ceremony. It seems so arcane, so mysterious. The planning sheet immediately puts them at ease and acquaints them with their options as to special music, hymns, and personal innovations. Most couples become visibly relaxed and enthused.

From the pastor's perspective, it provides a quick, clear explanation. Normally, it takes no more than ten minutes to walk the couple through the planning sheet. I figure this approach has saved me hundreds of hours over the years.

After we discuss the content, I reconfirm the times for the wedding and the rehearsal, double-checking my own calendar and having my secretary do likewise with the church's master calendar. I then lay out the schedule of events. My rule of thumb is that the sanctuary should be clear forty-five minutes before the ceremony. For example, if a wedding is scheduled for 1 P.M., the schedule would be:

10:45–11:15 A.M.: Party arrives and dresses.

11:15 A.M.–12:15 P.M.: Photographs.

1 P.M.: Ceremony begins.

The rehearsal is normally best held the night before, for the convenience of out-of-town participants. My recommendation is to set it early, about 6 P.M. Because people are notoriously late to rehearsals, I ask them to be there fifteen minutes before we plan to begin. This means the rehearsal dinner can begin at a reasonable time. It also means a busy pastor can get to bed at a reasonable hour — maybe!

I also advise the couple on who should attend the rehearsal: the wedding party (groomsmen, bridesmaids, flower girl, ring bearer, and ushers), both sets of parents, the organist, other musicians, and the vocalists.

When the schedule is agreed upon, I ask the couple to repeat it back to me.

The next item I arrange is the appointment of a wedding coordinator. A wedding coordinator is by no means a big-church luxury; this person is essential if the pastor is to be a good steward of time. Many smaller churches I know have a volunteer wedding coordinator. But if such a position is not possible, it will still be to your advantage to appoint someone to help coordinate the rehearsal and wedding — traditionally an aunt, relative, or some friend experienced with weddings.

This person performs three important functions. First, she

advises the bride as to the church's policies regarding music, the use of candles, photography, the sound system, dressing rooms, and even the cleanup expected. She can be of help in suggesting florists, caterers, dinner sites, and the myriad other details involved in a wedding. Second, she presides at the wedding rehearsal along with the pastor. Third, she coordinates the wedding plans, and thus takes much of the pressure off the bride and wedding party.

Finally, I suggest to the couple that a nice way to spiritually prepare for their wedding is to read the Psalms in reverse order as a countdown to their wedding day. For example, if there are ninety days until the big day, read Psalm 90, then the next day Psalm 89, and so on. My wife and I did this before our wedding, and we enjoyed these poetic expressions of praise. Couples have told me, "It was great to know we were both reading the same things each day."

The session is concluded with a time of prayer — and a reminder to bring the wedding license to the rehearsal.

The Rehearsal

Here's the typical agenda:

Greeting. I invite everyone to the front rows of the church. I introduce myself and briefly share my perspective that weddings are times of reverential worship and joy and that *both* are my goals for the ceremony. I also give a quick overview of the rehearsal agenda.

Prayer. I lead the wedding party in asking God's blessing on the service, reaffirming the purpose of the ceremony.

Introductions. I then introduce the wedding coordinator, expressing appreciation for her work and competence. She presides over the remaining introductions.

Instructions. The coordinator reviews several important items. She restates the *time* of the wedding and the time everyone must be there, and she asks the group to repeat it back to her. She offers reminders for *dressing*, telling the men, for instance, that when they pick up their tuxedos, they should try on the suit and the shirt to check the fit and should also make sure the tie, cuff links, suspenders, and shoes are included. Groomsmen and bridesmaids are shown their respective dressing rooms after the rehearsal. She gives advice about *posture*, including the warning about locking the legs and instructions to the men to keep their hands at their sides and smile.

Lastly, the coordinator displays her "Emergency Kit" (a carry-all bag). It contains "everything experience has shown us people forget," she says with a smile. "What do you think is in here?"

With some good-natured joking, she describes the contents: thread (selection of colors), needles, pins, shirt buttons, thimble, pin cushion, scissors, nail file and emery board, nail polish, hair spray, bobby and hair pins, comb, mirror, talcum powder, tissues, breath mints, aspirin, antacid, small first-aid kit, capsules of ammonia, static cling spray, lint clothes brush, cleaning fluid, pen, pencil, plain envelopes, name tags ("in case you forget who you are!"), all-purpose glue, cellophane tape, masking tape, matches, and tape measure.

Perhaps the real purpose of the Emergency Kit, however, is to assure the nervous couple they are indeed in good hands, and they can relax and enjoy the occasion.

We then walk through the entire ceremony. Afterwards, the bride and groom, the maid of honor, and best man meet with me to sign most of the wedding certificate, leaving only a couple of signatures for the next day.

The Ceremony

As pastor, I have always made it my business to be present during those forty-five minutes before the wedding to soothe frazzled nerves and complete the signing of the marriage documents. My role is to be calm and unflappable, to care for the couple, reassuring them everything will go well, and remind them their role is to enjoy this moment.

But even more, I am there to pray separately with the groomsmen and bridesmaids, inviting God's blessing on the moments to follow, asking that he will preserve in their hearts and minds the sacred ambience of the candlelit sanctuary, the radiant faces of well-wishing family and friends, and the joy of love exchanged in holy commitment.

During the ceremony, my role is to remind the people, by word and bearing, that this is a worship service. I try to guard against talking too fast or saying the familiar words in a perfunctory manner. Wanting this to be a personal experience, I speak directly yet conversationally to the two people in front of me, not to the crowd behind them.

I also make creative use of silence, which we so rarely enjoy these days. For instance, I prefer no music at all when the bride ascends the platform, so everyone can hear the rustle of the dress.

Then the couple repeats solemn vows very similar to those said by their parents and ancestors, thus affirming their solidarity with the past and their fidelity to the high call of God.

I'm sometimes surprised but always delighted by how my attention to a few details during the preparation, rehearsal, and ceremony can release the couple from nervous tension. When I am able to move a couple's thinking from anxious performance to tender worship, I feel I've accomplished my pastoral role.

WEDDING CEREMONY PLANNING SHEET

PRELUDE
  Time prelude begins: Time candles lighted:
SOLO/SPECIAL MUSIC (optional)
SEAT MOTHERS
AISLE RUNNER (optional)
PROCESSIONAL
PRESENTATION OF BRIDE
WELCOME/CALL TO WORSHIP
  Example: *We are gathered here to worship God and to witness the marriage vows of ___ and ___ (full names). Let your light so shine before people that they may see your good works and give glory to your Father who is in heaven. Let us worship God.*
CHARGE
  Example: *___ and ___, marriage is an honorable estate whose bond and covenant was instituted by God in creation. Our Lord Jesus Christ adorned and beautified this holy estate by his presence and first miracle at a wedding in Cana of Galilee. It signifies to us the mystery of the union between Christ and his church. And the Holy Scripture commends it to be honored among all people. Therefore, no one should enter this state of life unadvisedly, lightly, or wantonly; but reverently, discreetly, advisedly, soberly, and in the fear of God; duly considering the causes for which matrimony was ordained.*
CONGREGATION SEATED
DECLARATION OF INTENT
  Example: *"___, will you take ___ to be your wife, and will you be faithful to her, love her, honor her, live with her, and cherish her, according to the commandments of God in holy marriage?"*
  "___, will you take ___ to be your husband, and will you be faithful to him, love him, honor him, live with him, and cherish him, according to the commandments of God in holy marriage?"
PRAYER
ASCEND PLATFORM
HYMN or SPECIAL MUSIC (may go *before* ascending platform)
SCRIPTURES
  Examples: Gen. 2:18–24; Eccles. 4:19–21; Matt. 5:13–16;

John 2:1; Eph. 5:21–33; Col. 3:12–17; I John 4:7–12; Song of Songs 8:6, 7.

HOMILY (7–10 minutes)

VOWS

Example: *"I, ___, take you ___, to my wedded wife, to have and to hold from this day forward, for better or for worse, for richer or for poorer, in sickness and in health, to love and to cherish, and according to God's holy plan, I give you my love."*

"I, ___, take you, ___, to my wedded husband . . ." (as above)

RING

"___/___, what token do you give of your love?"

"A ring."

"___, with this ring I thee wed, and with all my worldly goods I thee endow; in the name of the Father, and of the Son, and of the Holy Spirit. Amen."

PRAYER

Example: *Bless, O Lord, these rings to be a symbol of the solemn vows by which this man and this woman have bound themselves to each other in holy matrimony, through Jesus Christ our Lord. Amen.*

DECLARATION

Those whom God has joined together let no one put asunder.

PRONOUNCEMENT

Example: *Forasmuch as ___ and ___ have consented together in holy wedlock, and have witnessed the same before God and this congregation, and in so doing have given and pledged their vows to each other, and have declared the same by the giving and receiving of a ring, I pronounce them man and wife together, in the name of the Father, and of the Son, and of the Holy Spirit. Amen.*

LIGHTING OF CHRIST OR UNITY CANDLE (optional)

VOWS OF THE CHRISTIAN HOME (optional):

Depending upon God for strength and wisdom, we pledge ourselves to the establishment of a Christian home. Together we will constantly seek God's will and honor Christ in our marriage.

PRAYER (kneeling)

SOLO OR SPECIAL MUSIC (optional)

KISS

RECESSIONAL

Part II
FUNERALS

S I X

PREPARING THE CONGREGATION FOR DEATH

Few of us have been trained to prepare congregations in any substantial way for the assaults of our final enemy, death.

RICK MCKINNISS

In seminary the rallying cry of my circle of classmates was "Life-giving ministry!" We were determined to extend that ministry in all circumstances and against all obstacles.

When I got into my first pastorate, however, I encountered three funerals in the first four months. And a terminal case of cancer was slowly killing one of the key lay leaders. Suddenly my rallying cry seemed incomplete. I needed to prepare myself and my congregation to face death.

I shared my frustrations with various colleagues and discovered to my surprise that many of them could tell similar stories. They felt the same concerns I did, but few had been trained to prepare their congregations in any substantial way for the assaults of our final enemy, death.

It helped, as I studied the Epistles, to find Paul himself came late to realize the need to prepare a congregation for the loss of fellow members, family, and friends. Believers at both Corinth and Thessalonica were badly shaken by the deaths of some of their members before the soon-expected return of Jesus. Both groups had questions and concerns. Had they correctly understood the gospel message about the resurrection and the promised age of blessing? And, if more deaths were to be expected before Jesus should return, what pastoral practices ought to be instituted? Such questions, if left unanswered, threatened to undermine these congregations he had worked so hard to establish. So Paul found it necessary to prepare both churches for the certainty of more deaths within their ranks.

As usual, I have found Paul's response a good one to follow. Paul begins to prepare the Corinthians and Thessalonians for death by laying a theological foundation.

Laying the Theological Foundation

I have become convinced this is exactly where our preparatory work must begin, and it is probably best done *before* tragedy is confronting a congregation.

Death is a metaphysical issue, a theological issue. Indeed, for most people, it is *the* theological issue. Folks who want nothing to do with theology — "Boring," "Too dry," "I want something practical" — automatically shift into theological high gear when death intrudes into their lives. People want answers that will enable them to carry on when they have been sent reeling by the death of a loved one. Death demands a theological response.

This would be easier if we could start from scratch, but almost everyone in my church already has an operational theology of death. This theology may be well-studied or gathered from clips of conversation when Grandma died. It may be grounded in Scripture or in pop psychology paperbacks. But no matter how hurtful or sub-Christian some of these lay theologies may be, it's important to proceed with care in replacing them with a healthier, more Christian theology of death.

In my first year of ministry, one of our church's heroes of the faith was struggling with terminal cancer. Many people in the congregation were troubled by the extent of the suffering she was forced to endure. Most troubled, naturally, was her husband, Rudy. During one visit he echoed what others in the congregation had said more than once: "God has some purpose in Katherine's death. I know he's going to use it in a great way. Otherwise, why would she be forced to endure such agony day after day?"

My first instinct was to challenge that notion. I don't believe God's actions are meaningless; nor do I doubt that he or we can carve meaning out of tragedy. But I'm quite certain we can never fully interpret the meaning of anyone's agonizing death this side of eternity. Even if we *can* see a beneficial outcome from someone's death, this theology of "God is using her death" has a side that darkens many people's faith. What goodness can we see in a God who employs such terrible means to accomplish his ends?

Fortunately, I bit my tongue that afternoon. Some wise Voice whispered against the arguments I was fashioning: *If you take this away from him now, what comfort will he have at the prospect of losing his life partner of fifty years?*

I began to see that taking the wrecking ball to people's theologies would tear down not only their ideas but their feelings and hopes as well. Through teaching and preaching, I was going to have to build patiently for them a new theological framework, one that would join faith and reality. I believe this framework includes three main concepts.

The foundational concept is the goodness of God. If Scripture teaches anything about God, it teaches that he is good. If people are to love and trust God in times of grief, they must be convinced of God's goodness. So it's become my practice whenever I make a statement about God — whether about his sovereignty, his justice, or even his wrath — to include in some way the message that our God is good and to be trusted. More than once I've told my congregation, "If I had only one sermon to preach, I would preach the goodness of God."

The second key concept is that death is evil. That seems obvious enough, but I find many lay people saying things like, "Death is a part of life. Dying is as natural as being born." Scripture declares that death and pain and grief are unnatural, contrary to God's intentions for his creation. Paul refers to death as an enemy. Jesus came to conquer sin and death and hell. To be sure, for the Christian, death is the experience by which one passes into eternal life, but Scripture would have us view death primarily as an ugly and painful intrusion into God's creation.

Grieving people know this only too well already. It's when we deny that death is evil that we hurt them. Richard, a friend and fellow minister, lost his daughter Sarah a few years ago. Only five years old, she died of unexpected complications from a simple virus. Richard and his wife grieved deeply and openly. Many people in the community of faith were uncomfortable with Richard's openness; they chastised him because he called the death of his daughter tragic and senseless. "When I call the evil thing good, or a tragedy a blessing, I'm not telling the truth," he told me in exasperation.

Not that Richard was without hope. "My faith in the goodness of God enables me to cope with this tragic loss," he told me. "Because of that faith, I have hope I will one day see Sarah again."

That expression of hope is, of course, the crowning piece of any theological framework that enables a congregation to deal with death. "Christ has indeed been raised from the dead," Paul tells the Corinthians, and in this mighty event is the promise of our own resurrection to eternal life. My congregation, like the one in Corinth, tends to forget this remarkable truth. I'm sure it's because I don't trumpet it frequently and fervently enough. A recent event in the life of our church convinced me of that.

One of our members, a young, healthy mother of three, contracted an extremely virulent cancer. Martha's doctors gave her a 5 percent chance of survival. When this was announced to the church, the congregation was devastated. The week after the announcement, we canceled adult Sunday school classes and gathered all the adults in the sanctuary to express feelings and to pray. During this time, one wise woman said, "What is happening to Martha is a terrible thing.

If she is not miraculously cured, she will die. But we do have a hope beyond this world. The Lord has promised us a place where there is 'no more death or mourning or crying or pain.' Regardless of what happens to Martha as a result of this illness, this is a hope she can live on forever."

That word was not new to any of us that Sunday morning, but it was a word from the Lord in season. It called us, troubled as we were, to believe our unique belief, to hope our unique hope. It was not unlike the words Paul shared centuries ago with two troubled congregations in Thessalonica and Corinth. Belief in the goodness of God, and hope, based on his victory over death, give the people of God a theological foundation, a place to stand when facing the onslaughts of the final enemy.

Educational Programs

But at some point theology demands a methodology.

I've found few packaged programs to help prepare a congregation for death. Publishing houses are not altogether unlike the pastors to whom they sell their wares; most of us would rather think about life than death. There are, however, some intentional things a congregation can do to help its members prepare for the experience we'll all face.

The obvious, and perhaps best, strategy is to treat the topic in Sunday school lessons, youth group programs, and Sunday services. One of our members is a sociology professor at a local college. Mike specializes in several areas, including the subject of death and dying (he has been known to answer when called "Dr. Death"). Mike put together a six-week adult Sunday school elective called "Dealing with Issues of Death and Dying" that focused on stages in the grieving process, how to comfort one who is dying, how to comfort the bereaved, what is important in planning a funeral. The class gave people not only information but the chance to talk about our culture's most taboo subject.

Obviously, we were fortunate to have a resident expert.

There are, however, some curriculum packages available that deal with similar issues. David C. Cook's Lifestyle Course, "If I Should Die . . . " provides excellent resources for the non-expert to lead a class on this topic.

One of the best things Mike did with his class was take a field trip to a local funeral home. The trip was not hard to arrange; it is the rare funeral director who will turn down an opportunity to have local folks come through. While at the home, the group discussed how to arrange a funeral and what the funeral should accomplish. The experience helped people, while in a noncrisis situation, prepare for their next visit to the funeral home, whether in the role of one bereaved or one comforting the bereaved. Such a visit is also valuable for youth groups, and even for elementary Sunday school classes.

Another way to help children begin thinking about this issue is for parents to take them to visitation sessions or funeral services for people to whom they are not intimately related.

Several years ago when an elderly lady in the congregation died, I suggested to my oldest son, Mark, that he come with me to the visitation. He agreed. On our way to the funeral home I prepared him for what to expect — family members weeping or talking quietly, the flowers, the casket with the body in it. We rehearsed what he could say to the bereaved family members: "I'm sorry that Mrs. Sturm died." We talked about what my role would be that evening and the next day at the funeral. On the way home Mark and I talked about what he had seen and heard and felt.

There are many other things a church can do to help its members prepare for death. One summer our church sponsored a weekly study group using Rabbi Kushner's *When Bad Things Happen to Good People* as a springboard for discussion. The author's perspective was certainly not Christian, but the best-selling book raised issues timely for our congregation; many members at that time had parents or other family members who were seriously ill. The group provided a forum to construct together a Christian framework for dealing with death and, more important, it provided support for those already grieving anticipated losses. Some members of the group still speak about the significance of that summertime experience.

I know a congregation that did a six-week Sunday evening series on preparing for death. Rather than preaching on the topic, the pastor used short case studies[1] on death-related issues, had a married couple talk about a "near-death experience" when their canoe capsized on a white-water expedition, and arranged a presentation on making a will by a Christian financial consultant (nearly half of all people in this country leave no will). For six weeks the topic of death and dying was on the front burner for that congregation. That series triggered dinner conversations, stimulated reflection, and helped a wise pastor share the load of grief counseling for many years to come.

A Context for Grieving

Some of the most significant preparations for death, however, involve not scheduled programs or instruction but the context for grieving. If people in the congregation do not feel free to express honestly their hurt and feelings, the most orthodox theology and the best curriculum will help little when death strikes.

Our church has long provided a time for sharing in the morning worship service. Tears are no more out of bounds during this time than is laughter. Real hurts, real doubts are expressed, as are real joys and real triumphs. I confess that when I first came to the church, this time made me a bit nervous. But soon I realized this sharing session announced to everyone present that real life and real faith can coexist.

This prepares people for death in several ways. A key one is it reminds us that some of life's experiences are bitter pills to swallow. We ought to expect that some experiences, even with all the resources of our faith, will be endured only with great difficulty. I recall hearing a Christian author tell about suffering a miscarriage quite late in a pregnancy. The next day her pastor stopped by with these words, "I know that because of your faith you're going to do just fine."

I contrast that story with one I heard from Gary, a member of my church, when I returned from a recent vacation. Gary had been conducting a week-long basketball camp for high school boys, and during the opening moments of the first day of camp, one of the campers had a seizure. Gary performed CPR, but despite his efforts, the boy died in his arms.

After the ambulance had gone and the family had been notified, Gary called some members of his home growth group and asked for prayer — both for the boy's family and for himself. He told me later, "I must have had a dozen phone calls or visits that evening. People shared; they listened; they ministered. I've never gone through anything so painful as watching that boy die, and with you on vacation, I didn't know who to turn to. But you should be proud of this church. They came through!"

Creating this caring climate for grieving people can happen in many ways. The type of sharing we do on Sunday morning won't work everywhere. In a colleague's church that is a bastion of reserved Norwegian Lutheranism, a context for healthy grieving has been fostered through the congregation's involvement with the local hospital's hospice program. Several key organizers of the program were from this church; they recruited volunteers within their congregation to minister to those dying and to comfort their grieving families. In a church with several hundred members who are senior citizens, this involvement has helped prepare the congregation for death.

Crisis Responses

Sometimes the best preparations for death come through our last-minute responses in the midst of a crisis.

Earlier I mentioned our decision to cancel adult Sunday

school classes and hold a group session for prayer the week after the congregation learned of Martha's troubling prognosis. This decision was made with her permission and full support. The time allowed the church to support Martha and her family in prayer and to stand with one another in the midst of the fear and faith, confidence and confusion, hope and hurt we all were feeling. Out of that session and visits with Martha and her husband has grown a prayer group to meet with them each week for the duration of her illness. The group is praying for God's healing intervention, but they also stand prepared to give encouragement and comfort should the illness progress and death occur.

Another time when a last-minute response helped prepare our congregation to face death came on (of all Sundays) Easter morning a few years ago. We had planned about as high a service as one can pull off in a Baptist church, and I had honed my sermon to a razor's edge. Just before I was about to ascend to the pulpit, I was handed a note: one of our members had taken a turn for the worse and was not expected to survive the day.

Alice was held in high-esteem in our congregation. Just about everyone in the church had a half dozen "Do you remember when Alice . . ." stories to tell. We had watched a debilitating case of Alzheimer's disease strip this fifty-nine-year-old woman of nearly all her adult capacities. But few people in the congregation knew Alice had entered the hospital Friday afternoon, let alone how close she was to death.

I wrestled with what to do, then decided to scrap almost all my sermon. I announced the grim news and invited one or two people to lead prayer for Alice and her family, many of whom were in the service. Then I began to preach an Easter sermon out of the deeply felt grief of the moment and spoke of the risen Savior who invites us to share in his conquest of the grave. I didn't have any well-polished points or dramatic illustrations. Nor did I have quick answers to the "Why?" I read on the two hundred faces. I just tried to point the congregation to the One who was raised from the grave that first

Easter morning. I asked them to reflect on what he had accomplished for Alice and for the rest of us who believe.

They were shaken; so was I. But those few, unprepared responses helped us face the death that did indeed come that afternoon. Though last minute, those actions were life giving.

Congregations need to be equipped to face the trauma of death with both realism and faith. With proper preparation, congregations can discover that even our final enemy is unable to kill a lively faith or deaden a life-giving ministry.

---

1. Many cases are available through the Case Study Institute, The Intercollegiate Case Clearing House, Soldiers' Field, Boston, MA 02163.

SEVEN

PASTORAL CARE FOR GRIEVING FAMILIES

What do we do when death calls? We — the church — come alive!

PAUL L. WALKER

On Thanksgiving Day, 1980, our family gathered at Grandmother's house in Tennessee. We laughed, sang, and played with uncles, aunts, and cousins. Extended family had come from all over, and we felt a special closeness on this perfect day of fellowship and reunion.

Thirty-six hours later I received a phone call.

"Reverend Walker," the voice began, "I'm sorry to inform you that your wife and son have been involved in a serious head-on collision. Julie will recover, but your son was killed. Where do you want us to send his body?"

A dull ache washed over me. *It can't be true!*

In a terrible moment, the joyous closeness of Thanksgiving changed to the empty loss of death. Paul, my first-born, was gone. Paul, who had just finished his master's degree and was beginning work on his Ph.D., this son who had brought nothing but pleasure and pride. *Tell me there's been a mistake!*

For thirty-two years in the pastorate, I'd had to help families grieving the loss of a loved one. I had thought often on the question, "How can I best help these hurting people?" It would seem, then, that this personal loss would be more easily understood and handled.

Not so! As I felt so deeply when my son died, the death of a loved one is agony. There are no textbook approaches, no easy answers, that will take away the pain, but we can offer help to people who are facing the worst hurt of all: death.

A Faith Approach to Death

Our own view of death will inevitably be conveyed in our relationships with those experiencing death. As Christians, then, there is no other alternative but to bring a faith approach to our ministry to the grieving. And this approach provides the only true comfort and help.

Death is inevitable, universal, unpredictable. It affects us all. Further, death is almost always accompanied by fear. It is hard for us actually to conceive of death as possible; to see life really ending; to think in terms of finality, loss, and emptiness.

We often associate death with all things bad and negative. We don't like to use the word *death*, so we talk about "going to be with Jesus," "passing away," "meeting the Master," "crossing the divide," or "receiving our reward."

Yet the Bible addresses death openly and provides us with a way to overcome it. When someone in the congregation dies, the grieving family and I return again to the Scriptures' wisdom. In the biblical view, life on earth is temporary. It is depicted as a shadow, a weaver's shuttle, a handbreadth, a vapor. The Bible makes it clear that real life is eternal life. Death, overcome by Christ, brings timeless life. For believers, it is not to be feared. We are triumphant in the resurrection of Christ.

In every encounter with those experiencing death, we bring this faith approach. This is the uniqueness of our Christian experience, and it can be conveyed through our words and actions. This is not smugness, but we come with an abiding confidence that through the hurt, emptiness, and ache, we can emerge in the power of the Christian faith.

For the bereaved there is always the question, *Why?* Why did this occur? Why did God let this happen? I have found it helpful to focus instead on the question, *What?* What can we expect from God? This concept seems to have therapeutic value for those whom I have counseled.

We can expect God to work for good in all things. This is the universal promise of Romans 8:28. While everything that happens to us is not necessarily good in itself, under the direction of the Father, every situation blends together for a symphony of ultimate, eternal good.

We can expect God to finish that which he has begun in our lives. This is the promise of Philippians 1:6, rendered by one translator as "He will put his finishing touches on you." In the time of trouble, our faith may seem small, but God will nourish it until it grows to the size he desires. We will someday be glorified because God completes every work he begins.

We can expect the Spirit to intercede for us. Paul makes this clear in Romans 8, adding, "If God be for us, who can be against us?" God acts on our behalf.

I saw the power of this faith in the Whitmire family. D. J., the husband and father, died suddenly from a heart attack the evening before he, his wife, and his son were to join the Mount Paran Festival Chorus for a Christmas choir trip to Israel. The once-in-a-lifetime trip included singing at Manger Square in Bethlehem on Christmas Eve before an international television audience.

Such a sudden death was naturally a tragic blow to the entire church. In this case it had special significance since Stan, the son, was the piano accompanist for the Chorus and could scarcely be replaced at such a late date. I wondered for them, *What do you do when tragedy strikes just when you are packing to take a trip designed to fulfill a lifelong family dream?*

Sure, Martha and Stan were crushed; they grieved; they felt the loss and emptiness of death; but they also found inner resources through the power of faith. They remained behind one day, attended the funeral and the interment, then joined the group in Jerusalem and finished the tour. Martha wrote me a note following the trip:

The way God's love comes through others amazes me. From the Thursday night three weeks ago until today, I have not felt alone. Maybe briefly, but not for very long. God, through someone or something, shows me his love.

After we arrived in Jerusalem, I woke one morning with the song "Unfailing Love" on my mind. I sang it. For about three days, that song kept going through my mind — on the bus, walking with the crowd.

The Israel trip was certainly the right thing for us. Leaving here wasn't easy, but we felt the Lord was in this trip from the beginning. We still hurt, but this same God who's been so near won't leave us now.

Thanks again for your love and support. Please continue to pray for us.
Love in Christ,
Martha

Ministry to families when the deceased did not know Christ becomes more difficult. In these cases the faith approach focuses on the family that remains. I spend extra time with the grieving family following the funeral. I try to help the family gain a sense that God is going to see them through. "There are many things we don't know or understand," I may remind them, "but there is only one thing you can do now, and that is to leave the situation in God's hands."

An Empathetic Approach to Grief

A second key aspect in ministry to the grieving is genuine empathy. Only then can we be truly helpful resources in the time of grief.

Bereaved people may describe their grief in a variety of ways, but they all feel acute sadness, irreparable loss. It's not unusual for grieving people to complain of physical problems or to have a preoccupation with the image of the deceased. Often there is a sense of guilt, hostile reactions, restlessness, even assumption of characteristics of the deceased.

In all this, we want to help in three areas. One, we want to aid the person's *transition* from the problems of separation back into the mainstream of life. Two, we try to caringly help the person *accept* the hurt, the loss, and the emptiness. The grief process is a natural, necessary response to death. Those who do not honestly face the loss run the risk of delayed severe emotional reactions. Three, we seek to help family members *confirm* their faith. Our resources for these tasks include, primarily, prayer and the Word, empathetic listening, and counsel.

In my experience, this ministry involves several stages.

1. *Relationship building.* My first task is to let the person know I am *really* interested in his or her problem. As pastors, we are so busy that it is easy to be preoccupied and unwittingly show it through our posture and listening behavior. So right at the start, I want to communicate by words and actions, "I want to enter your private world, understand your hurt, and help you deal with it."

2. *Exploration of feelings.* Then I want to encourage people to express how they feel. Grieving people often feel guilty, angry, numb, or resentful. People may say to me, "I feel cheated by what God's done to me." I've found people won't admit these feelings if I haven't first built a relationship with them and then given them verbal permission to express these emotions.

3. *Interpretation of the feelings expressed.* I was counseling a man whose wife, an alcoholic for twenty-two years, had just died. The woman had gotten drunk one evening, as usual, and the man had helped her to bed and tucked her in. Later he found her dead in her sleep. The man felt a terrible sense of guilt, thinking he was responsible for her death. "It's my fault," he told me. "I should have known what was going to happen." These feelings of guilt and responsibility for the death, though unrealistic, are powerful. When my son died, I kept thinking, *If only I had asked him to spend another night!*

The counselor can help the grieving person see that these feelings are rarely realistic. None of us knows what is going to happen.

4. *Determining possible alternatives.* At this point, we help

the person think of the choices available. "Do you feel ready to go back to work?" "Would a vacation be helpful?" "Have you considered living with your mother or sister for a few weeks?" Once the various options have been listed, the person needs help thinking through the strengths and weaknesses of each.

5. *Helping people follow through.* Once a decision is made, people in deep grief sometimes need help carrying it through. When my dad died, my mother stayed with us for two weeks. Then she decided it was time to return to her home in Florida and resume her activities. For a few days, I called her each morning and said, "Mom, what are you going to do today?" That gentle but firm call helped her do what she had decided.

Yet even our best efforts to facilitate the grief process may not be well received. There are always those who become bitter, resentful, and hostile.

I remember one family whose daughter died after an extended illness. The family established a memorial fund. Because our church is large, we've had to set a policy that we will advertise such a fund or scholarship for four weeks only. We announced the fund frequently during that period, and people in the church gave generously.

But it wasn't enough. One year later, the family wanted the girl's picture displayed on the Communion table and a special offering taken. Without authorization, they called Sunday school teachers and committee leaders and told them to take up offerings for the fund. They held several garage sales, and many people in the church helped them. But then I would see the girl's mother in the church hallways dressing down someone who hadn't helped.

Finally it had to be confronted. I met with the parents and let them know their demands were unrealistic and their behavior was hurting others. They have attended only occasionally since, and the breach has never been satisfactorily repaired.

Regardless of a person's response, however, we are called to be facilitators, to help people as they "walk through the valley of the shadow of death."

A Caring Approach to Details

When death calls, the bereaved face a myriad of details. They have to think of cemeteries, burial lots, funeral homes, caskets. They need to contact family and friends, determine the funeral service format, arrange music, set schedules, take care of food for the family. Good pastoral care helps lift the burden of these details.

To do so, however, means that we, too, must attend to many practical details. Through the years, our church has established a procedure that seems to work well most of the time. When we first learn of a death, we do the following:

1. *Alert the appropriate support groups.* In most cases the person and family involved will be part of a Sunday school class, one of our choirs, or a small group of some kind.

Support groups are also coordinated by neighborhood to provide a meal for the family. The Ladies' Auxiliary pays for the meat, and neighborhood people provide everything else. The church office arranges for flowers to be sent to the family.

2. *Initiate pastoral care.* I or another pastor will meet with the family, offering to be available for counseling, helping with calling family members, or any other needs that may arise, such as helping to select funeral home services. Walking into a room filled with caskets can be devastating to the bereaved. Sometimes they want me simply to be there with them. I may clarify the different options available or help them decide what they can sensibly afford to spend.

3. *Arrange the funeral service.* At some point the service itself is discussed. Once the time and place have been settled for the newspaper and public announcement, there is ample opportunity for detailing the final order of service. We have found this is best worked out after most relatives have been contacted and the initial shock has subsided.

We offer all the church resources available, which include accompanists, soloists, the chapel, and so on. At the same time, I watch that the grieving family does not overdo. The deceased may have had five favorite songs, and they want all of them played. Or the family may have known four or five ministers through the years, and they want all of them to have a part in the service. I try gently to guide them away from too much. I'll list all the elements they want in the funeral service. Then I may say, "Let's think this through. This service will run sixty to seventy-five minutes. I know how you feel, but my experience tells me that will be too long; you'll suffer too much." Then, perhaps, "These two songs are quite similar; perhaps just one could be played."

In some cases, I'll work with the family to outline three possible services, from simple to elaborate. Then I'll suggest they let them sit and come back to them the next day when they can think through the options more clearly.

My goal is to be flexible yet make the funeral worshipful and strength giving, regardless of the situation surrounding the death.

4. *Follow up.* Within ten days after the funeral, a personal letter is sent to the family and a follow-up visit is made.

Where there is persisting grief because of tragic circumstances, such as suicide, a child's death, or crime-caused death, counseling is arranged as needed over an extended period. The appropriate support groups are also called upon to keep in touch.

In the counseling process, I look for symptoms other than pure grief. In some cases, a grieving family member may have actually hated the deceased. When the person died, he had to act like he loved her, but now he must deal with his deeply buried feelings of anger.

I listen and try to understand the full impact of the separation. Often I work to relieve guilt feelings, and challenge the bereaved to renewed activity. Grieving people need work and activity as therapy. When my son died, I would lie awake in the middle of the night and think, *I can lie here and grieve myself to death or I can get up and do something.* Our house has never had such clean closets.

We may suggest to grieving retirees that they come work at the church for a while. There is always plenty of office work to do, and they are then busy and around people.

Beyond counseling, however, there is the *koinonia*, the church as the fellowship of the Holy Spirit. We try to keep in touch with the family through the various support groups, but, in truth, this is probably the weakest link in the chain. So often, we forget the lingering effects of grief. The caring friends, helping people, and supporting group return to normal, and on occasion, the grieving ones are overlooked. This always hurts when it is discovered, and it results in a continual reorganizing of follow-up procedures.

For the most part, however, the church as a caring community comes through. The Wells family's experience illustrates this. Pam Wells, a twenty-one-year-old member of our congregation, was an experienced hiker. While camping in Texas with a national hiking club, she was killed by a flash flood.

I had observed Pam's spiritual development over the years. Just a few weeks earlier she had shared a part of her diary with me:

> *I am writing this right after my psychology class. I feel the love of Jesus all over my spirit. I've just talked to another believer in Christ. The unity and communion of the Holy Spirit between two believers is so fantastic!*

I was traveling in the Pacific and Japan for the Air Force when it happened, so I was not able to be there personally for the funeral. Upon my return I received a letter from her father. Here is his testimony of invincible faith:

> *While you were out of town last week, we found the Lord sustaining us by his Spirit working through the Mount Paran staff and family in a most unusual way. Pam's death, of course, leaves us with a deep sense of personal loss. Our immediate response was, "Lord, give her back, please — she's only twenty-one!"*
>
> *But we found out on our knees, some hours later, that his thoughts are far above our thoughts and his will beyond our will, and in his perfect will he had called her home. So in the following early-morning hours we released Pam into the arms of Jesus Christ. It's not easy, but then, he didn't promise us a garden of roses.*

What he has done staggers and boggles the mind. Imagine! Eternal life beyond the grave! Truly no sting in death! Instead, a hallelujah chorus singing "To God Be the Glory!"

Yes, it's true. He's given us his assurance in his Word that he never forsakes us, even in our darkest hour and at the point of physical death. This assurance is undergirded by the fellowship of Christian brothers and sisters everywhere. We find this fellowship especially in our church.

What do we do when death calls? We — the church — come alive!

EIGHT

FUNERAL AND GRAVESIDE SERVICES

At a wedding, I may feel like a necessary accessory along with the flowers, rented tuxedos, and candles, but at a funeral, I sense people sincerely look to me for help. People are more open and responsive, appreciative of help given — more than at any other time.

CALVIN RATZ

I love funerals. Not that I enjoy death, it's just that I agree with Solomon, who said, "It is better to go to the house of mourning than to go to the house of feasting" (Eccles. 7:2). After talking and praying with the bereaved, I go home feeling I've made a difference; I've touched people at the point of their deepest need.

Burying the dead is part of pastoral turf. How we handle it goes a long way in determining our acceptance in a community and the depth of our spiritual impact on a congregation. Any strengths I muster can lose their power if I can't help people who are bereaved.

A well-handled funeral can be the best opportunity for genuine public relations a church and its pastor can have. It doesn't lead to instant church growth, but it breaks down barriers and builds an attitude of respect and appreciation. It's a positive point of contact with people who have drifted away from the church.

Whenever I've gone to a new congregation, I realize my first funeral is a chance to let the people see a side of me not obvious from the pulpit. Parishioners are initially skeptical about a new leader. They're wondering what the new pastor will be like and how much they can trust him. When they see me conduct a funeral service, people notice whether I care about them as individuals, even in their darkest moments.

Exciting and Exacting

These pastoral responsibilities are both exciting and exacting.

I consider them exciting because they provide opportunities to get close to people. At a wedding, I may feel like a necessary accessory along with the flowers, rented tuxedos, and candles, but at a funeral, people sincerely look to me for help. People are more open and responsive, more appreciative of help given during bereavement than at any other time.

Funerals are exciting, too, because of the opportunity to present the gospel to people who otherwise would not hear it. Seldom is there a funeral service without some non-Christians present.

Funerals are exciting because we possess a legitimate reason for hope and comfort. Many aspects of life and faith escape my grasp, but when I come to the graveside, I know I'm on solid ground. The Bible gives a sure hope. I don't need to waffle with sentimental clichés. I can speak with confidence to each member of the family.

But a funeral service is also exacting. I bury a person only once, and there's little forgiveness if I blow it. My pet fear is that when I do the committal service I'll forget the name or say the wrong name.

It's exacting because of the time constraints. Funerals usually come with little advance notice and, for some unknown reason, often during a busy time in the church calendar. There's scant time to prepare. Though funerals demand a certain precision, the time to make everything right is limited.

It's exacting because the congregation is often unfamiliar. Usually non-Christians dot the pews, and often relatives attend who are unfamiliar with our church. They don't know me, and I don't know them. I have to feel my way through, sensing the mood of the mostly alien congregation.

It's exacting because of the variety of emotions present. Fear, grief, cynicism, guilt, joy, anger, and relief are all present in a mix of helplessness and hope. I've discovered it's not always possible to anticipate how family and friends will respond during a service. Some who appear to have the strongest faith and greatest depth of character struggle most with death.

The Pastor's Role

I was surprised to find that nowhere in the Bible does it tell pastors to bury the dead. Yet when I was ordained to the Christian ministry, part of the charge given was to "bury the dead." The church and its leaders have quite properly accepted this responsibility and privilege.

Why don't we let professional funeral directors care for the dead? Why do we not only get involved but take a leading part in the events surrounding death? When someone dies, what can we do that no one else can do?

As a pastor, I have a unique perspective. I'm a friend, but I'm also in a position of authority. I'm close enough to "weep with those who weep" but removed enough to bring objective truth.

Schooled in the details of death, a funeral director is helpful because he knows the right ways to embalm, arrange flowers, and approach the grave. A pastor's job goes beyond getting the dead body into the ground with decorum. I offer both faith and friendship to the living — those grieving people looking for help. They need someone calm to hold their hands; someone who can offer them hope, not sentiment; someone close enough to feel some of the pain. As a pastor, this is my role.

For this role, I need a realistic view of life and death. I've learned to accept the inevitability of death. I *am* going to die; it's only a question of when. Further, I accept the temporary nature of all present relationships. I can't try to hang on to what God says won't last.

In addition, as a Christian, death is not something to be

feared but rather to be anticipated. Paul made this very clear. He told the Corinthians, "Therefore we are always confident and know that as long as we are at home in the body, we are away from the Lord. . . . We are confident, I say, and would prefer to be away from the body and at home with the Lord" (2 Cor. 5:6–8). He also said, "For to me, to live is Christ and to die is gain" (Phil. 1:21).

Since I'm not afraid to die, I can use death as an opportunity to share the gospel with the living, teaching the brevity of life, the importance of preparing for our own inevitable deaths, and the good news that God will comfort those who sorrow.

What do I want to accomplish when there's a death? I approach funerals with three basic objectives. First, I want to get the surviving family through the days surrounding the funeral. Second, I want to get the dead person appropriately buried (or cremated). Third, I want to get the gathered family and friends to think about life, death, and meeting God.

Pulling the Family Through

My involvement usually starts with the phone call that brings the announcement of death. I visit the family as soon as I can. At death, more than a person dies; a network of relationships ceases. So there's shock, disbelief, guilt, resentment, and a whole range of other emotional responses of those close by. My first priority is to hold their hands, let them cry, and give them support in a variety of ways.

Seldom do I start any funeral arrangements during this initial visit. If the deceased has just passed away, there's too much shock. It's too harsh to talk of caskets and burial plots in those first few minutes. I let them know that tomorrow is soon enough for those decisions, and I'll be back to help them then.

On my second visit, I try to build a consensus of what should take place at the funeral service. I prefer to have as many of the family members present for this as possible. I determine who is in charge and who is going to make the major decisions. Sometimes that isn't clear. I want to establish not only who has the right, but who, emotionally or through force of personality, is going to make the arrangements. At times conflict or disagreement within the family places me in a crossfire.

On one occasion, the widow, who had the right to make the decisions, was out of town, and I had to finalize arrangements for the service. By telephone she specifically told me what she wanted, but the sister of the man who had died came into my office and told me the widow's arrangements were inappropriate. I was caught between the strong feelings of the wife and those of the sister. It was impossible to come out a winner.

If there's a question about the decisions, I'll sometimes say to those gathered, "Now I know we are all involved and want to do what's right, but I understand Peter is in charge of making the arrangements. Peter, what do you think we should do?"

During this time, I observe how the family is coping with death. I try to distinguish between hysteria and grief, between legitimate sorrow and hopeless despair, trying to anticipate those who'll have emotional difficulty during the funeral. I watch nonverbal communication. Who's afraid to look at my face? Who walks out of the room when we talk about the service? This helps me avoid problems later on.

I pay particular attention to family photos and artifacts in the home. Asking questions about family photos is an indirect way of gathering useful information from families that aren't well-known. These clues help me personalize the service and counsel the family afterward. I jot them on a card either in the home or as soon as I get to my car.

For the service, I try to honor personal requests — a favorite hymn or passage of Scripture. I gather the obituary information or have one of the family write it up for me. Prior to the service, I verify the accuracy of my information and the pronunciation of names with someone in the family.

Primarily, however, I want to explain to the family the sequence of events and how they will likely feel during the service. I talk about the value of tears. Walking the family through the service in advance sets them at ease and enables me to accomplish more when the service actually happens. I let the family know that I will meet them before the service for a final word of prayer prior to entering the sanctuary.

I realize that at this moment, I'm in a position of great power and tremendous trust. I carry a spiritual authority that normally I am not given. The family is looking for help. They hang onto my words. I also realize I'm told things in the time of bereavement that are strictly confidential. People say things out of guilt or grief that should never be repeated. I'm careful to observe confidentiality.

I conclude this second visit with a strong but brief statement about the biblical perspective of death. I'm careful not to minimize grief, and may even point out how some Bible characters expressed their sorrow at the death of a loved one, but I do want to give a message of assurance and confidence. I sometimes read a portion of Scripture. I then pray with the family, thanking God for the memory of one who was loved, and asking God to sustain and comfort the family.

Burying the Dead

The dominant theme of a funeral service has to be that Jesus Christ is alive. Christ's death and resurrection supply meaning to our deaths. His resurrection provides a stream of grace that enables us to cope with grief. This message must be heard above all the emotion and tradition surrounding a funeral service.

I want the funeral service to help people get their eyes off themselves and their circumstances and onto God, who in his great wisdom and love has everything under control. Due respect and tribute need to be given to the deceased, but I want the service to witness to God's provision of life through Jesus Christ, who brings a whole new dimension to *living*.

I want people to feel I've prepared this service just for them. I've attended some services where the name of the deceased was not even mentioned. It's obvious the words had all been said before for someone else. I definitely want those grieving to know I share their sorrow and genuinely want to help.

At some time during the service, I speak directly to the key members of the grieving family by name: "Mary, you've been through a lot. This has been a great shock. You had a wonderful husband. I want you to know God will help you in the days ahead. My prayers are with you." Of course, this is what we're trying to do with the whole service, but I find saying the person's name gives the message impact.

At times I ask someone capable of public speaking to make remarks about the life of the deceased. This is particularly helpful for those situations where I haven't known the person. When I know the person well, I try to go beyond giving the essential facts by recalling positive experiences. For example: "I remember visiting Dorothy both at her home and in the hospital. Though she knew she had cancer, she never seemed to doubt her faith or feel regret. She had strong courage even though she was aware of what was happening. She spoke only of her concern for her children."

There's even a place for humor, although not jokes. Death is serious, but brief, tasteful remembrances of humorous events can break the tension and bring a sense of release. At one service an eldest son brought tribute to his father. He mentioned several serious qualities and then concluded by relating how his father had always chided him for leaving the bathroom messy. This middle-aged son ended his remarks by looking up toward heaven and saying, "Dad, I just want you to know I cleaned up the bathroom before I came to your service." In some services, such a comment might have been out of place, but that day it fit. It helped the family get through the day.

Obviously, I'm as positive about the deceased as possible. There's something good to say about everyone. But several years ago I learned I had to be honest. I was preparing for the funeral of a man I didn't know. I was gathering some biographical information from his grown daughter. She simply said, "Please don't say a lot of nice things about my father. I

75296

loved him, but he was not a good man. If you say he was good, people won't believe anything else you say."

The cause of death and the person's character or "credentials" determine the type and tone of the funeral service. Services for prominent church officials, well-known pastors, and former missionaries tend to involve more speeches of tribute and are more structured. During such services, I fight to control time by giving specific time limitations.

A service for a known unbeliever or someone who has lived an unwholesome life is much briefer. The emphasis of the service shifts from giving thanks for the deceased to providing comfort and encouragement to the bereaved. This is particularly the case in the death of a non-Christian spouse. I say little about the deceased. Rather I focus on how God will help the believing partner who remains.

In services for elderly, well-known church members, I'll often make the emphasis one of thanksgiving for a life well-lived. For one man who had been active in the ministries of the church until the time of his death, I used Hebrews 11:13 as a text: "All these people were still living by faith when they died." It was an opportunity to speak of his involvement, his acts of kindness, and his faith in God that remained strong for a lifetime.

I vary the sequence, but somewhere there's a hymn, usually a solo, and, depending on the circumstances, a few comments on the life of the deceased. I always include a message based on Scripture. I pray at least twice during the service, once asking for the Lord's presence and help during the service, and once asking for the Lord's counsel, comfort, and wisdom for the grieving family. I don't allow the prayers to become either minisermons or counseling sessions. I make them short and conversational; flowery language and theological jargon don't make sense to the sorrowing family.

I base my encouragement in Scripture. I shy away from sentimental poetry. I'm a preacher, not a poet. The underlying thought I want to leave is that the Bible provides solid answers about life and death, and Jesus Christ provides meaningful support to those who grieve.

The logistics of funerals and burials vary greatly. There's certainly no right or wrong way, only what's appropriate to the situation and community. My job is to provide the necessary outlet for legitimate grief.

The Graveside Service

The traditional burial following the funeral service can destroy the positive tone established during the service. Many people have told me the burial service was the hardest part of their grief experience. The big struggle was to walk away from the grave. So I suggest having the burial *before* the service to relieve the family of some of this pressure and to free them to hear the comforting words of the service.

If the burial service is for just the immediate family, the time at the graveside becomes more personal and family oriented. The service in the church or funeral chapel can then conclude on a positive note of hope and encouragement. In addition, relatives and friends are available immediately following the service to support the family; they don't have to wait till after the burial.

I tell the family the graveside part of the service is short, so they're not surprised by its brevity. Depending on the mix and number of people present at the graveside, I may have them sing a chorus or verse of a familiar hymn to involve them in the burial, helping them express their grief and affirm their faith. The overriding word at the graveside is *resurrection*. Since the grave is but a temporary resting place for the body, I don't dwell on the end of life but the hope of the resurrection.

Following my benediction, I greet each member of the immediate family individually by name. I don't say much; it's just a final personal touch. I then quickly withdraw and leave the family alone. They need private time to say things they might feel uncomfortable saying in my presence.

Speaking of Life and Death

The heart of the funeral has to be the sermon. A funeral message isn't lengthy, but it should be long enough to provide substance for faith to grasp. I aim for a ten- to twelve-minute message. I try to make my style conversational. There's no place for the bombastic, the flamboyant, or the spectacular.

Regardless of my text, I include a brief statement of what happens when a person dies, how God helps those who sorrow, and how we can prepare for our own eventual deaths. I have a congregation at a funeral that I don't have any other time. I don't abuse the privilege, but I've concluded that outsiders feel cheated if, as a man of God, I don't tell it like it is and say something of substance.

I recently went through an unusually hectic three weeks. In addition to a number of other pressing situations in the church, I had five funerals. Yet I preached a new and different sermon at each service.

How did I find time to prepare five new funeral messages? Several years ago I accepted the fact that death is going to happen, and I will be called upon to conduct the services. Further, I've learned that since funerals don't happen at convenient times, I have to be ready before I'm asked to perform them. So I keep a file of potential funeral texts. Perhaps calling it a file is a little strong. It's really just a folder with scraps of paper on which I've scribbled a potential text and a seed thought or two. When I'm called about a death, I go to my folder with possible texts, and usually there's an appropriate one to give me a place to start.

I tend to stay away from the most obvious texts. On the other hand, I try to stay away from obscure texts. A funeral message is too short to give background information and explanation. People want something familiar. They need to fasten their faith onto what they know.

The underlying message of every funeral service is hope. Believers can have assurance and confidence in facing the grave. As a pastor, I bring divine help to enable the family to cope with change, loss, and the process of rebuilding.

Following the Service

After the service is when ministry is often most needed. Immediately following the service, the women of our church provide a luncheon. This relaxed time gives family and friends an opportunity to express their concern and love to each other. It's the start of the healing process.

Sometimes during these informal gatherings we've had a time when folk were encouraged to make some personal comments about the deceased or family members. This was particularly moving following the death of a young lady, Elfrieda, who died in her thirties. Many people told how she had blessed their lives. One girl spoke of how Elfrieda had brought her to the Lord. This was not only a fitting tribute to Elfrieda, but brought healing and release to those who participated.

I let the family know I'm available to help. There's a follow-up visit to assess the situation and determine ongoing ministry. I make sure there is public prayer for the family during the first Sunday service bereaved family members are back in church.

In addition, I seek to connect each bereaved person with someone in the church who can befriend and encourage in an ongoing way. Pearl was widowed about three years ago. Today she is reaching out to another widow, who is struggling. Pearl phones her each morning, meets her often for coffee, and sees to it that she gets to church. This continuing ministry of comfort is too great for me to handle, and not my sole territory anyway. Godly women like Pearl minister in ways I can't.

Three women approached me recently following a funeral service for a friend. They paid me the compliment that I'm sure has been given to many other pastors: "Pastor, we hope you stay in this church a long time, because we don't plan to die for several years. But when we do, we want you to preach our funerals." I had passed their test.

NINE

SERVICES FOR PEOPLE YOU BARELY KNOW

It's not unrealistic to hope the service will lead a good number of those present into the presence of God.

MARK COPPENGER

Is her name Carrie Mae or Carrie Lou? My stomach tensed as I stood to give the funeral message. *I can't believe I left the name off my notes!* My heart beat fast. I reached into my jacket pocket as discreetly as possible. *Where's that obituary? It's soaking up the sweat that's spreading under my arm. It's so damp it's stuck in there. Looks like I'm going to have to do the message with all pronouns — "she" and "her" rather than using her name.*

I looked at the family, seated in the first few rows. *Will they suspect I've forgotten the name of their loved one? Should I ask them quietly for the name? Should I stop and fumble to get this damp obituary unstuck from my pocket?*

I wish I could tell you this was fiction, but except for the name, it's not. My first year in the pastorate included thirty-one funerals, and often I strained to get the names straight. I'd write them in the margins of my Bible. I'd rehearse them in the "green room" at the funeral home. But now and then, I'd find myself stuck with pronouns. I felt like a duck, trying to move serenely on the surface while paddling like crazy underneath.

It's just not easy ministering to people you barely know. Usually the scenario goes this way: Your secretary hands you a note on the death. As you're rushing out the office door, she calls out, "She's Robert Caulkins's sister-in-law."

"Who's Robert Caulkins?"

"Bud Freely's nephew. He used to work for Axworth Drilling (*Who? Robert or Bud?*) before it became Shambling Pipe and Valve, which went bankrupt in '56."

"Okay. Thanks. Got to go."

You sit in the home with strangers all around, except for one older lady you met at the adult Sunday school Christmas party. It's hard to imagine doing anything particularly helpful for these people, and there seems to be the possibility of doing some harm — either through an ill-chosen phrase, a forgotten name, or just a general failure to rise to the occasion.

Fortunately, you don't remain a novice for long. And as I've done more of these funerals for people I've barely known, I've discovered they can be gratifying. In fact, they're often not as difficult as those for long-time acquaintances with whom you share a vast store of personal memories.

After all, the expectations of the family and congregation aren't as high. They know the constraints of time and your unfamiliarity with the person. If there were months to prepare the funeral, then they'd expect a substantial research program of you. But the folks know you've had to scramble, and they can be forgiving.

Compare this to the funeral of a giant of the church, well known to you and everyone. The "you'd better get it right, Buster" factor is quite high in this case. You enter the pulpit on these occasions with the suspicion that when you're done, a brief silence will be followed by a display of score cards like the ones competitive divers face. But when they know you and the deceased were strangers, they're more inclined to leave the cards down.

None of this is to suggest our primary concern in preparing a service is reputation. We have important things to say as God's people on the scene. If offense and disappointment are the natural outcomes of being faithful to God in the funeral setting, then so be it. But offense due to ignorance is nothing to be cherished, and it's nice to know you're going into a situation in which the chances for it are reduced.

Eulogy

In funerals for the little known, the eulogy terrain is treacherous. It's difficult to get a candid picture of the deceased. As people sit in the parlor with the pastor, they feel obliged to limit their remarks to niceties. I suspect if it were Hitler's funeral, little or nothing would be said about the Holocaust, but someone would be sure to praise his special work on behalf of Aryans.

It's often said that funeral directors are prime candidates for religious cynicism since they hear so many scoundrels preached into heaven. Day after day they observe pastors gloss over corrupt lives in an effort to make everybody feel good, and so the meaning of discipleship is obscured. If for no other concern than the souls of funeral directors, we should be careful about heaping up misplaced praise.

It's embarrassing to hear after a funeral full of eulogy that the person was, in fact, a skinflint and a tyrant at home. As a pastor, you realize you've jeopardized one of your most precious vocational resources, your credibility.

The danger extends to praise of family members. I once ventured some kind words for the widow, calling her "one of God's good gifts" to the man. I knew this would be gratifying to her and felt sure, in light of the affectionate words I'd been hearing, that it was true. But not long after, a man in the community took me aside to inform me that she was the worst thing that had ever happened to her husband; she had tormented him with suffocating advice most of his life. The man's tone let me know he counted me as just one more in a long line of ministerial saps. G. K. Chesterton built his "Father Brown" detective series around the premise that clergy are savvy folks since they have access to so many dark secrets, but the notion that pastors are fuzzy idealists is strong, and a misdirected eulogy serves to reinforce this crippling impression.

There is danger as well in the opposite direction. What shall we call the pronouncement of critical words at a funeral? Mallogy? Kakalogy? Antilogy? Whatever the term, there may be the urge to wax prophetic against the departed and his type. Here lies before you a perfect sermon illustration for the "rich young ruler" or the "Demas has departed" texts. Only kindness and a strong desire to preserve your ministry and life will keep you from preaching it. Outright condemnation is rare at funerals.

But, as those of us who've written reference letters know, in a context where flowery speech is the norm, a meager word of support says a great deal by what it leaves out. This is fine; it communicates with delicacy. But even here I hesitate.

Before I risk damning with faint praise, I consider that the relatives may have been the reticent sort. Or perhaps they weren't morally or spiritually observant. They told me nothing bad, perhaps, but their failure to tell the good could be leaving me with an inaccurate impression. If I'm not careful, I'll pass along that impression to the funeral congregation. In short, a eulogy can underdo as well as overdo it.

It's embarrassing to be patronized by a relative after the funeral: "If only you had known her better" or "It's so hard when you don't really know them." The tone tells the story: "You really fouled up, but I'm going to make a lame excuse for you just to keep things pleasant." You know you've under-eulogized.

So I shy away from eulogy. It's so easy to get it wrong. If it was unavoidable, it would be worth the risk, but there's an alternative. I don't have to eulogize. Neither do I need to stick to a purely generic funeral, just leaving a blank for the name. Let me call this alternative the "personalized" funeral.

Personalizing the Gospel

I begin by scavenging, searching for bits and pieces of information about the person. As soon as possible, I go to the home where the family is gathering. I have them talk about the person, giving each one there a chance to reminisce. Often friends and neighbors will add to what the family says. Certain themes emerge. Anecdotes generate anecdotes. There is a pause for tears, and then a fresh word comes. Sometimes it runs fifteen minutes, sometimes an hour. I may ask questions to open new regions of memory. All the time, I'm taking mental notes.

Many families bring out objects to show you — a poem stuck in his or her Bible, a Sunday school class history, a photo of a long-dead spouse, a newspaper clipping, a watercolor he did. Any one of these can supply the key to your funeral remarks.

Back at the church are other resources for those at least remotely related to the church. Long-time members can add information. Bound issues of the church paper may hold other traces. I keep a file folder on each household in the church. Into these go letters, hospital visitation note cards, newspaper clippings. When death occurs, I pull the family file. Perhaps there's a Christmas card I'd forgotten, a notice of election to a civic club office, or the record of a comment made from the hospital bed.

I'm not after a comprehensive presentation of his or her life. If so, then the day or two between death and the funeral would be filled with anxiety. There would be too much to discover and assimilate. That's why I steer clear of eulogy; it presses me into this sort of anxiety.

But when the focus is not on the person but on the Lord, the bind is not there. I simply try to use an item from the deceased's life to introduce a truth from God, not build a case for the person's glory. Thus I scavenge with a different spirit. I'm not looking for everything but for something, some hook upon which to hang an apt biblical word.

Some examples:

1. Checking her hospital visitation card, I found I'd once read Psalm 121 to Alice. At the funeral, I recalled that moment together and then focused upon that psalm.

2. As I visited in the home, the family showed me a poem

placed under the glass on Margaret's dresser. The closing words, "Remember God the Gardener knows when flowers need the rain," provided the base for comments on the sufficiency of God's grace for the woman who'd died — and for those of us who remained.

3. The family made clear Jack's love for the Bible, sports, and music. I saw in all these a hunger for heaven, where we find, respectively, the full truth of God, release from drudgery, and a new song. The message was not upon what a good fellow he was but upon the nature of heaven.

4. Bill's son passed on to me a small metal cross with the words "Jesus Christ" written on it. He'd found it in his father's effects. At the funeral, I mentioned this by way of introduction to the truth of the Cross.

The son also told of a time when Bill flew across country to help him after a car wreck. From the report of this deed, I quickly moved to a description of God's sacrificial love for his children.

Notice that in none of these was there a serious attempt to praise the deceased. In fact, in the first one, there was no praise at all. But the simple act of tying a biblical point to some feature of the deceased's life personalized the message and prepared those gathered to receive it.

You'd think this minimal attention to the glories of the deceased would frustrate the family and friends, but it's my experience that this approach is well received. Family members will sometimes coach you on what to say on their loved one's behalf, but they, too, seem satisfied with personalizing rather than eulogizing. Once they've seen the Lord and his work lifted up, they realize this is something better than what they had in mind. You might say they discover what they wanted all along, though they didn't suspect it.

The juxtaposition of loving reference to their dead friend and words of instruction from God is generally satisfying and helpful. Of course, when it comes to working with people, there are no foolproof methods. I've also blown this approach a time or two.

Shortly after coming to a church, I was called to do the funeral for a woman. I wasn't sure what I could say about this near stranger, but as I visited the family in her home, I found she had been a pretty good artist. It struck me that a sermon could be built on this interest of hers.

In brief, the message went this way: In art, we have the realists (e.g., Roman sculptors) and the idealists (e.g., Greek sculptors). The Bible is that way. It shows the realism of David's sin and Peter's denial, the warts of human existence. It also shows us the ideals, the perfection of Jesus and heaven. So God meets us at every level. He takes us from perdition to sanctification, and so on.

I cringe to recount it. It's so strained. You can almost see the beads of sweat form on the words. If I'd taken more time to reflect on what needed to be said, I could have made a more direct and satisfying statement. Having taught aesthetics for a number of years, I saw a chance to trot out some old course material. And it sounded like old course material trotted out. I determined to serve up better baked bread thereafter.

The personalizing approach helps keep me clear on what I should count success. Have I succeeded when the family is gratified and failed when they're not? Not necessarily. If so, then flattery, touching both the deceased and the family, would be the best percentage shot. But I can aim higher.

It's not at all unrealistic to hope the service will lead a good number of those attending into the presence of God. When this happens, lives are changed. Comfort, repentance, quickening can occur, or at least get underway. In the personalized funeral, this happens as we establish rapport with personal reference and then move on to God.

Ready for the Good News

We don't think of funerals as laughing matters, but it's hard to keep from smiling when you see some of the folks who attend them. People who never come to church, whose lives are as dissolute as any to be found, find themselves seated before a preacher. They're usually black-sheep family members or rough-edged fellow workers. Whether they exhibit the florid face of the lush, the smug impatience of the self-made man, the hair and jewelry of a lounge lizard, the eyes that match a drug-fried brain, or the affected sophistication of the socialite, they look lost. Some squirm in borrowed Sunday-go-to-meetin' suits. Others posture in expensive, dress-for-intimidation outfits. And there you stand with Bible in hand. If you'll pardon the expression, "What a setup."

You see these people at most funerals, but you see more of them at funerals for those you barely know. The reason you barely know some folks is they are virtual strangers to the church. There are, of course, other reasons for unfamiliarity. You may be new to the church, the size of the congregation may be great, or the deceased may have lived elsewhere in recent years. But in many cases you're dealing with the unchurched.

A clear statement of the gospel is in order. I use a simple presentation I've committed to memory. It touches on repentance, trust, and the lordship of Christ, and provides a scriptural base for its claims. It's the sort of thing I could share in a moment with a desperate man. I want to be able to leave that funeral with a conviction like Paul's: "I am innocent of the blood of my listeners because I've not hesitated to proclaim God's counsel" (Acts 20:26–27).

If the personalizing item does not lead directly to the gospel statement, I introduce it in other ways. If I do compliment the deceased a bit, I might say he was no fool in that he did not rely on good qualities or deeds to make him right with God, which is an impossibility anyway.

On other occasions when I was assured the deceased loved the Lord, I've presumed to speak for the dead, telling the congregation the one thing he or she would most want them to hear, namely the gospel. No one has objected that I've misrepresented someone's interests.

A well-handled funeral can put pastors in a unique position. Because we have played a critical role in a delicate situation, we enjoy a special standing with the family. They see themselves in our debt. We're pasted in their book of memories. We can therefore move more easily into their lives to do God's work. Are they lost? They might give evangelistic counsel a hearing. Are their lives in disarray? Perhaps they'll open their door and ears to advice. Are they hoping for help for a friend or relative? They'll likely think of the one who helped them in their time of difficulty.

So many walls encircle the Christian minister. When breaks occur, when opportunities for entrance show themselves, then there's cause for celebration. Funerals for those we barely know can serve this cause admirably.

TEN

HANDLING THE HARD CASES

For all the good things we can do for families in the hard cases, we can do just as many bad things — and that's the challenge.

ROGER F. MILLER

It was the kind of situation that gives clergy tremors.

A local funeral director called me to arrange a graveside committal service for a former resident of our community. I didn't know the person. He had been living halfway across the state for many years but had relatives still in town who were marginally connected with our church.

"The service will be simple," the funeral director said. "Just some Scripture readings, words of committal, and a prayer. Only the immediate family and a few old friends will be at the cemetery."

The wind at the cemetery whipped the trees and tested the ropes securing the burial canopy. Topsoil from the plowed field adjacent to the graveyard blew into our hair and the creases of our clothing as we waited for the hearse and the cars carrying the family.

The appointed hour came and went. No body, no family, no motorcade — but people, lots of them! The "few old friends" that began gathering ten minutes before we were due to start had swelled to a crowd of over a hundred. One person said to me, "I'm so glad they're having a funeral service here. I wasn't able to see the family earlier." Suddenly the brief committal service I had prepared seemed woefully inadequate.

I also noticed many of these so-called old friends weren't so old. In fact, they were nearly all in their thirties or early forties. Through some delicate conversation with one of them, I discovered they were contemporaries of the deceased. *This is no old man at the end of his natural life!* I thought.

Pulling the funeral director aside and whispering as quietly as I could, I began a vigorous interrogation. Why hadn't he told me a large crowd would be showing up expecting a full funeral? Why didn't he tell me the deceased had been in the prime of life? What other little surprises awaited me?

"I wasn't in charge of the original arrangements," he protested, "just the burial. I'm as off balance from this as you are." I had worked with this funeral director enough to know he was sincere, but our mutual ignorance was little comfort.

Just then the procession of vehicles made its way through the cemetery gates, nearly an hour late. As the hearse and family cars moved between the rows of markers, I asked the deceased's aunt, standing next to me, what had happened to this young man. Over the howl of the wind, she replied, "He shot himself."

Out went the funeral service I had been mentally preparing to replace the original committal service. As the cars came closer, I worked feverishly to formulate a service that would speak specifically to the people affected by this man's death and the circumstances surrounding it.

The man's widow, her parents, and in-laws got out of the cars, and I could see their grief was intense. As I greeted the family, I quickly picked up that their grief was compounded by guilt, so common among the survivors of a suicide. The funeral director opened the casket (apparently the man had shot himself in the chest), and those present filed by to see him lying there, a bottle of his wife's perfume in one hand and a bottle of something else in the other. I did not doubt this impromptu funeral would be the toughest I had ever done.

What Makes Hard Cases Hard

In over a decade of pastoral ministry, I have officiated at nearly three hundred funeral services. The very first was for a young woman killed in a car wreck on a twisting Kentucky road. Two weeks prior, we had celebrated her graduation from high school. Two of the more recent services I've had were for an elderly lady, also the victim of a car accident, and her husband. The husband had been driving the car in which she had sustained her fatal injuries. A combination of guilt over the accident — he was at fault — and the feeling he couldn't live without her led the man to borrow a neighbor's car keys on the pretext of running an errand, get in the car, turn on the ignition, and poison himself with carbon monoxide. It's natural, I suppose, but of all the funeral services I've performed, the ones I remember most are the "hard cases."

Death comes through many doors. For some, it slips through the door marked "merciful healer" and liberates a person from pain, illness, and a worn-out body. In these cases, death makes sense; it's easy to see how death fits naturally into the cycle of life. Any death certainly produces grief in those who survive. A natural death following a long, full life, however, tempers grief's pain with the achievement of a life well lived and a smooth transition from one life to another.

Then there are times when death bursts through the door marked "obscene intruder." It comes as a vicious thief who robs the victim and family of health, happiness, and much of the abundant life Christ taught was God's intention. These deaths are untimely — suicides, accidents, murders, terminal illnesses, or stillbirths. These deaths take babies, children, young adults, and those in middle age. These deaths make no sense; they frustrate any attempts to provide tidy answers when hurting people ask *why?* These are the hard cases.

I remember the funeral I did for a young man who seemed to have everything going for him — he was an accomplished professional chef, he had a good marriage, and he was expecting a baby soon. However, like Richard Corey in Edwin Arlington Robinson's poem, this outwardly successful man had found something in himself with which he could not live. One fall evening he took his brother's deer rifle to a tree stand outside of town and shot himself. As it happened, the brother who owned the rifle arrived at the scene just in time to hear the gunshot.

Funerals for suicides are difficult not only because of the grief heavily laced with guilt but because of the societal and ecclesiastical attitudes toward death by one's own hand. How are we to handle the funeral of a suicide if we are taught — and believe — that to kill oneself is sin?

Deaths by automobile accidents are difficult because they are untimely. Often a sense of unfairness shackles the loved ones. The bitterness was almost palpable at the funeral service of a popular young police officer from our town who was killed one summer night when his car flipped and hit a telephone pole. Because the officer was so well liked, the funeral was huge, and as I talked to people at the service, I detected less an asking of why it happened than a basic rage that it did.

Increasingly we give pastoral care to families of people who have succumbed to AIDS. From the most recent information, AIDS will continue to claim many lives. Since most victims of AIDS are homosexual males, at these funerals we encounter deep negative feelings toward the homosexual lifestyle. Add to this the fear AIDS has caused among the general population and the double burden parents often carry, adjusting not only to the death of a child but also to the newfound knowledge of his sexual orientation, and the combination makes for a truly hard case. In the one AIDS-related funeral situation I've been in, I did as much counseling with the parents regarding homosexuality as over the death of their son.

Funerals for babies and children confront us most graphically with unfulfilled dreams, dashed hopes, and unrequited love. I started 1985 with the funeral of a stillborn infant delivered New Year's Day. It was a terrible despair I felt as I stood at the podium next to a tiny white casket and tried to comfort a desolated family. I thought of my own two children and how I would feel if one of them died.

The Challenge of the Hard Cases

Few ministerial duties provide as great a challenge and opportunity as these funerals. In a hard case, the funeral becomes more than a ritualized leave-taking from the deceased. When done effectively, the bereaved can experience firsthand a sense of God's care and concern. This caring cuts through the worst pain and provides the strength to withstand it. People can feel free to be angry with God, secure in the knowledge their anger will not drive God away. They can express their feelings, knowing they will survive the pain. Ultimately, those who go through the most difficult grief experiences may emerge stronger in their faith with the aid of good pastoral care. That is, of course, if we do our job well.

For all the good things we can do for families in the hard cases, we can do just as many bad — and that's the challenge. Poorly given, ministry can have a definite counterproductive effect on those in grief, actually damaging the emotions and spirit. The bereaved may feel estranged from God and the church family just when closeness and nurture is needed most. When grieving people perceive any insincerity on the part of the pastor, they tend to think, *The minister doesn't care; God must not either*. The grief process may thus be arrested for a considerable length of time. Symptoms of grief such as anger, guilt, and a sense of loneliness may be intensified.

Not long ago the director of our community mental health agency asked me to talk with a young staff member whose father had died two months previously. She told me that in reaction to his grief he was making work difficult for clients and the rest of the staff. I talked with the young man and found he was distressed about the anger he was venting on everyone. He revealed that the minister who served the family during his father's illness and funeral seemed more concerned about the details of the will and the settlement of the estate than about the pain of the family members. No doubt this young man was angry about other things as well, but his anger increased as he perceived the awkward ministry to the family as a lack of caring.

What to Avoid

In difficult funerals, what is most effective becomes clear when we consider what should be avoided.

Don't be the "answer man." A mystique surrounds our work, much as in the field of medicine. We spend years of preparation and more years of practice to answer life's most basic and imponderable questions.

It feels good to have people seek us out for answers. When we are confronted with a hard case, however, there are no easy answers. Nothing we can say or do will bring back a dead son or reverse a car accident. No answer we give will make a suicide easy to think about.

Recently I read a sermon a fellow minister had delivered at the funeral of an AIDS victim. The thrust of the message was that this untimely and tragic death was perfectly understandable — it was God's punishment for the victim's lifestyle. I wondered: *Was this "answer" to the question of why this young man had to die really helpful to the family and friends left behind?*

We must rid ourselves of the notion we can fix painful situaations by providing answers to questions that are unanswerable.

Don't treat this as "just part of my job." Some time ago I sat with the family of a dying woman. Prior to our hurried summons to the hospital, she had been proceeding along a normal postoperative course of recovery. Her vital signs looked fine. Then a weak spot in her aorta ruptured. There was nothing anyone could do. As her blood pressure dropped dramatically and her pulse faded, her family and I sat silently together in the waiting room, bound to one another by our feelings of shock and helplessness.

With us sat another minister, pastor of the church where

one of the woman's daughters attended. I had called him at the daughter's request so he could lend emotional and spiritual support to her. What he did instead was fidget in his chair and glance frequently at his wrist watch. When the woman finally died and the daughter, disgusted despite her grief, told the minister he could leave, the clergyman compounded his mistake by offering to stay longer. The daughter icily informed him that wouldn't be necessary. It was a long time before that woman went back to church.

I don't believe the minister acted as he did because he didn't care. Rather, I believe he behaved that way because he was feeling as uncomfortable as the rest of us. It would have been far better to acknowledge his discomfort at the outset and let the rest of us support him while he supported us at the same time. He certainly should have refrained from the false offer of further assistance, which came off sounding forced.

At the funeral, don't give a canned presentation. Recently I took an informal survey of the funeral directors in my area to check their perceptions of clergy effectiveness in problem funeral situations. Their responses were discouraging, to say the least.

One funeral director told me, "It seems as if most of the ministers come in with a service that's cut-and-dried no matter what the cause of death. For every service they use the same Bible passages, the same prayers, and the same messages. It's almost as if they don't care." Virtually all the other funeral directors echoed the sentiment.

This disturbs me. If the funeral directors are sensing a lack of caring on the part of the clergy, what must the families be feeling? Do they think we are there just to perform a perfunctory service, an empty ritual? Since feelings are magnified by grief's pain, I wonder if the people who need us most, those in the hard cases, feel angrier, guiltier, and lonelier for our having been a part of the process.

I sat through the funeral of a suicide victim in which the minister made no mention of the suicide and said the name of the deceased only once. The rest of the service was read out of a book. I felt as if I had been led to the table but denied permission to eat. It's true that different medicines work for different ailments, and no one drug can cure every sickness. It is no less true that a canned funeral service that takes no consideration of the unique circumstances of the death will seldom be helpful to people hurting in a hard case.

I believe we resort to canned services because of our discomfort; the prepared, impersonal service appears an easy way out of the situation. We become far more effective in handling the hard cases when we allow ourselves to grieve along with the bereaved. The best thing we can do as we prepare for each difficult funeral service is to ask ourselves what it is that gives us the most courage and strength, given the way we feel about the situation. It is as true in ministry as in anything else: we work best with what we know and have ourselves experienced.

What We Can Do

So what can we do?

The funeral service is the place where we can define the boundaries of grief. We acknowledge the loss of the deceased, we recognize the feelings we experience as a result of the loss, and we offer hope that this most terrible time will pass and we will be able to affirm life as good once again. With that in mind, there are several things we can do.

Tailor the service to the family at hand. The message that worked for the loved ones of the "church grandpa" will be ineffective for the family of the child who succumbed to leukemia. When preparing the service, I try to keep the family and circumstances in mind. If possible, I get to know something about the deceased and his or her family prior to the service. How the person died will, more than anything, determine the cut of the funeral service as I tailor it to the needs of those attending.

Mention the cause of death. Earlier I wrote of the services I did for the woman who died in the car accident and her husband who committed suicide as a result. As I began the second service, I said something like this:

"Ten days ago, we gathered here to receive God's strength and comfort as we acknowledged the loss of Betty Wilson. Her death in an accident left us shocked and hurting. No one felt the pain and shock more than her devoted husband, Hank, and so, tragically, three days ago, Hank ended his own life near his home."

With that opening statement, I immediately established the unusual circumstances that brought us together. It frustrates a family when a pastor talks all around the cause of death without addressing it directly. In some cases, the circumstances will be obvious, as in the death of a child. In other cases, however, part of our effectiveness lies in enabling the survivors to admit "John was killed in a car wreck" or "John was murdered," or even "John killed himself." Mentioning the cause of death gives everyone present the chance to start recovering from grief from a more-or-less common starting point.

Of course, I need to exercise sensitivity and care, and discuss plans with the family ahead of time. In the case of the man who committed suicide, I checked with immediate family members before saying anything publicly. Since the circumstances of his death were common knowledge anyway, they felt it would be most appropriate to acknowledge the suicide. Given strong emotional attachments to concepts like suicide and AIDS, it is essential we discover the most tactful yet honest way to present the cause of death. In the case of the AIDS victim, I obtained the consent of the family before reading as a part of the obituary that he had died of Acquired Immune Deficiency Syndrome (that was honest, yet not so scary sounding as AIDS).

Acknowledge this is an abnormal time. This helps the survivors place their unpleasant feelings into perspective. Often, a grieving person will feel as if he or she is losing touch with reality. Time and again I've had surviving spouses tell me, "I feel like I'm losing my mind. I won't be able to function normally ever again. I can't think straight and I can't remember a single thing."

Our honest acknowledgment can help the bereaved see this is something we do not normally encounter; it is a time for unusual feelings and reactions. There is good reason to feel spiritually and emotionally out of kilter when one we've known and loved dies suddenly and tragically.

This acknowledgment offers, too, the hope that feelings will return to normal once the worst of the grief is overcome. That in itself can be a great comfort to people who are thrown into a spiritual vertigo by a tragic death.

Allow for honest ventilation of feelings. The death of my father in 1981 was a pivotal experience in both my life and ministry. Dad died at the age of fifty-five from lung cancer. At my own request, I co-officiated at the burial service. When I made that arrangement, I had no idea how difficult the service would be. I stood at the grave facing my family and friends and invited them to share my feelings, feelings like the writer of Lamentations when he wrote:

> I am the man who has seen affliction under the rod of his wrath; he has driven and brought me into darkness without any light; surely against me he turns his hand again and again the whole day long. He has made my flesh and my skin waste away, and broken my bones; he has besieged and enveloped me with bitterness and tribulation; he has made me dwell in darkness like the dead of long ago. He has walled me about so that I cannot escape; he has put heavy chains on me; though I call and cry for help, he shuts out my prayer; he has blocked my ways with hewn stones . . . my soul is bereft of peace, I have forgotten what happiness is. . . ." (Lam. 3:1–9, 17–18)

In the case of a murder, suicide, child death, or other difficult situation, certainly there should be anger. Often guilt or other feelings will manifest themselves. By reminding people these are a sign neither of mental instability nor a lack of faith, we can provide a place from which the bereaved can begin working back to where things are normal and life is good.

Emphasize God's presence. Even though grieving people may be angry at God to the point of rage, God's love is still important to them. The effective pastor is the one who can help the bereaved through Scripture, prayer, and message to know that God is present, not as the oppressor but as the comforter on the side of the oppressed. While we may not know why a fatal accident happened, or why a child contracted leukemia or a woman killed herself, we do know that God is present and on our side.

In addition to lifting up God's presence through the promises of Scripture, we may also point to God's presence as we find it in caring family members and friends. I have seen friends surround widows and others at the cemetery and infuse those hurting people with their strength through touches, hugs, firm clasps of the hand, and other expressions of caring. This is the most effective thing I've found to pass along to family members and friends of hard cases.

As pastors, we are physicians of the spirit. We bring talents, training, and special gifts to the hard grief cases just as doctors take their talents and skills into difficult medical cases. An openness to the guidance of the Holy Spirit, the sensitive use of the pastoral skills we possess, and a willingness to share the grief journey of those we serve can place us in partnership with God — who truly brings forth miracles in the hard cases.

Part III
SPECIAL EVENTS

 E L E V E N

INFANT BAPTISMS AND DEDICATIONS

Baptisms and dedications unite us all as children in need of our heavenly Father.

GARTH BOLINDER

T he Mother's Day dedication service was moving toward its conclusion. The last of the six beautiful babies was being presented to the Lord. Solemn questions had been asked the parents:

"Will you, by God's help, provide a Christian home for this child and bring her up in the worship and teaching of the church, that she may come to know Jesus Christ as her Savior and follow him as Lord?"

"We will," the glad parents responded.

"Will you, members of this congregation, be faithful to your calling as members of the body of Christ, so that this child and all other children in your midst may grow up in the knowledge and love of him?"

"We will," said the united congregation.

It was a holy moment. Many eyes glistened among the adults. Children looked on in wide-eyed wonder at this re-enactment of the ancient ritual. The infant Jesus was again in the Temple, Simeon looking for the consolation of Israel, Anna praising God.

As I pronounced the benediction on the last peaceful child,

holding her in my arms and softly repeating the words of blessing, "The Lord bless you and keep you . . ." suddenly she looked up at me, startled, with wide-eyed terror. Her face reddened and twisted into a grimace, a coil of anguish waiting to unwind. In the next instant, the entire sanctuary was filled with her piercing wail. This little beauty, cradled so gently in my arms, was howling directly into the microphone clipped to my lapel. So much for the holy moment.

Should I muffle the noise by holding her tightly against my chest? Or quickly give her back to her parents? Should I cry with her? Or laugh?

I started to laugh. So did the congregation. It wasn't the laughter of ridicule or embarrassment. It was a spontaneous, holy laughter in the midst of the fears and pains of life. Sarah and Abraham knew it at Isaac's birth. In Bethlehem's delivery room, so did Mary and Joseph.

Was this holy drama or human comedy? Maybe a little of both. As that baby was crying, the pastor fumbling, and the congregation chuckling, the story of salvation was being told once again with delightful clarity. A child had been born to a woman — another reminder of God's redemption through Eve's seed. The congregation — God's new covenant people — surrounded this little life with warmth, love, and joy.

But what about this intruder, this pastor who takes children from the security of parents' embrace, pronounces eternal words over them, and calls to one higher? A mere man or woman, whether draped with silken vestments or sporting a polyester leisure suit, becomes a formidable presence at this moment of divine initiation.

Common Ground

Are there not great lessons to be learned and common pastoral ground to be found in the midst of the theological turmoil that surrounds Christian baptism? I dare not presume to solve that age-old debate (though some might say, "What debate? It's truth verses heresy!"). As authors Donald Bridge (Free Church) and David Phypers (Anglican) point out in their provocative book, *The Water That Divides*, "One of our Lord's last recorded commands to his followers was 'Go . . . and make disciples of all nations, baptizing them in the name of the Father and of the Son and of the Holy Spirit' (Mt. 28:19). That his followers have, in general, obeyed his command is beyond question. . . . Yet despite this, perhaps no command of Christ has occasioned so much controversy, division, bitterness, and mistrust as this one."[1]

Still, in the midst of this continuing controversy, pastors of all stripes are called to welcome little children, to tell the grand story of redemption. We realize, whether through baptism or dedication, that children can play a major part, and the way we utilize such occasions can have eternal consequences.

Jesus and the Children

Even to the casual observer, it's obvious the gospel writers placed particular importance on Jesus' attitude toward children. Not only did he delight in them, they seemed to delight in him. There was a joyful fullness in their relationship that confounded both the skeptic Pharisees (as expected) and the faithful disciples. When everyone wanted to keep the children from Jesus, he bid them come and had some rather harsh words for those who hindered them.

Does the Bible assume what modern neonatal medicine is just now discovering, that infants have great capacity for awareness and perception? The story of John the Baptizer leaping in the womb of his mother as the prenatal Messiah approaches certainly causes us to wonder. As Frederick Buechner has pointed out, "When it comes to the forgiving and transforming love of God, one wonders if the six-week-old screecher knows all that much less than the Archbishop of Canterbury."[2]

In thinking of our pastoral role, whether in infant baptism or dedication, we must first focus on the tender relationship between Jesus and the children. What can be done to reflect his divine concern and love for them? Let's start with some practical considerations.

Know the child's name. As basic as this might sound, it indicates our pastoral attitude and involvement. No doubt we all issue some form of certificate for either baptism or dedication. It shows care as we get the proper names of the children and have the certificates neatly filled out well in advance. As a personal touch, we use several people in the congregation who do calligraphy. As I sign the certificates, I make a conscious effort to become familiar with, even memorize, the names of the children I'll be holding on Sunday. If our heavenly Father has every hair numbered on those little heads, then I figure I had better know the children's names.

Consider the logistics of the service. Most pastors I know try to include the children early in the worship service. This way anxious parents can be spared the trial of trying to keep down the din as the noontime feeding and nap approaches.

Set a caring tone. The pastor's attitude sets the tone for the families involved, the congregation, and, I believe, for the infants as well. With so many things going on, it's easy to inadvertently telegraph our busyness or preoccupation, which does not reflect the welcome of Jesus. So I find I must consciously bring to the ceremony a smiling face, a gentle voice, a firm yet tender embrace. These tell the children of a Love that will not let them go.

Music, prayers, and Scriptures can be chosen that emphasize the grace and peace of Christ. I suppose we could think of the rites of baptism and dedication as eternal lullabies, soothing with the peace of God helpless children thrust into a sinful world. An old poem by George Wither captures this mood:

Whilst thus thy lullaby I sing,
For thee great blessing ripening be;
Thine eldest brother is a King,
And hath a kingdom bought for thee.

The wants that He did then sustain,
Have purchased wealth, my babe, for thee;
And by His torments and His pain,
Thy rest and ease secured may be.

Thou has yet more to perfect this,
A promise and an earnest got,
Of gaining everlasting bliss,
Though thou, my babe, perceiv'st not.[3]

Be creative. Every time I hear the hymn "Loving Shepherd of Thy Sheep," I'm deeply moved, because that's the song Pastor Art Nelson sang quietly to our firstborn after baptizing her. Years later, when Pastor Wes Swanson held up our second child after baptizing her and declared, "Behold what manner of love the Father has given us, that we should be called the children of God," I realized a new dimension to 1 John 3:1.

I've talked to pastors who send personal letters to every baby they've baptized or dedicated — immediately after the Sunday ceremony, or later, on Christmas, Easter, or another significant date. Though initially read by the parents, these letters go into baby books and become spiritual signposts in later years.

I remember my daughter's excitement when she came home and told us that next week a special party was going to be held for her — in honor of the anniversary of her baptism. With all the secular paraphernalia that engulfs our children as they grow, maybe we should be looking for more creative ways like these to undergird eternal and spiritual realities.

Jesus and the Children's Parents

Let the little children come to Jesus, but insist their parents bring them. The Bible knows nothing of the individualism so popular in our time. Baptisms and dedications are opportunities for family ministry. I believe sensitive preparation of parents is both a theological and practical necessity.

I'll always remember a visit with a newer couple in the church. Both held doctorates from prestigious Ivy League universities. They were the epitome of success and style. They were also spiritually hungry because the birth of their first child caused them to reconsider their lapsed religious upbringings.

What a privilege to visit them one evening to discuss the pending baptism of their newborn. I admit I was a little awed by their academic and professional accomplishments. But they had wanted spiritual counsel. So I went.

"No," I replied to one of their questions, "we don't believe the Scriptures teach that baptism guarantees salvation."

"We don't either."

"Well, can you tell me about your personal faith in Jesus Christ?"

What followed was a thought-provoking time of discussion and testimony about new life in Christ. They had recently entered that life and wanted to witness to the grace of God through baptizing their baby. If I had bypassed the visit, either through casual assent to their request for baptism or by skepticism at their spiritual status, I'd have lost a rich occasion. The family would have missed reflecting on the meaning of their newfound commitment. And the congregation might have lost the privilege of enfolding this family into our midst.

While it may not be possible to cultivate a deep relationship with every set of parents, I do work hard to integrate parents into the baptism or dedication process. Personal contact with parents helps them understand the significance of what they are desiring for their child. It affirms the necessity of their own profession of faith, dispels any misunderstandings that this is the completion of their spiritual responsibility for their child, and prepares them to answer with integrity in the service the questions of their faith and intent. Such personal involvement also helps cement my future relationship with them.

As a church becomes larger, finding time for all this is a genuine problem. But to me, the bigger problem comes when we neglect such a wide-open door to ministry.

The grievous sociological climate of our day quickly presents us with unusual circumstances here. There are no easy solutions to the complications that divorce, sexual permissiveness, blended families, and single parenting bring. Yet when a parent comes to the pastor, concerned about the spiritual welfare of his or her infant, what an opportunity to counsel the parent about the true meaning of the gospel, of repentance, of forgiveness, of a life of obedience!

Teaching and Witness

Kimberly's tiny body was bound in a cast from the abdomen down. As I held her in my arms and gazed into her eyes, I marveled at her oblivion to her serious condition. The drama was not lost on the congregation, however, nor on Kimberly's parents. They realized that after casts came a series of surgeries that might correct the birth defect. If the surgeries were not effective, this child faced the life of a paraplegic. Her baptism that Sunday morning had a marked impact on the entire congregation. I didn't realize how much until later in the week.

A couple called me for an appointment to talk about the baptism last Sunday. Since they were new to the church, I guessed they wanted to discuss (or argue) the theology of baptism. *Oh well*, I sighed, *one more time around.*

As the conversation began, I realized I had prepared for the wrong subject. They didn't want to talk baptismal theology. They wanted to talk about personal faith — their lack of it, to be exact. During the baptism of this little girl in her half-body cast, this couple was deeply moved. They began to cry again as they told me about it.

"It was as if that little girl were a symbol of our lives," they said.

"There she was, crippled and bound, yet glowing with happiness and peace in her father's arms. When you took her and spoke of Christ's love for her — that he died for her sins — that was more than we could take.

"Later it hit us. This little girl could grow into a joyful, fulfilled woman even if she never walked. She could learn to survive and thrive in the world. There are thousands of people who illustrate this, but that baptism showed us the one thing that she could not do for herself."

"What's that?" I asked.

"She can't save herself. Only God can."

Somehow, during the liturgy of presenting a child to God, of proclaiming the grace of God, of praying for that child in Jesus' name, the Holy Spirit had convinced this couple of their need for Jesus Christ. Though I was deeply moved as I held that frail child in my arms, I was too intent on balancing the baby to think of any further spiritual impact. But the impact was there.

Why is my faith so small? Jesus pointed to children and said they illustrated the values of the kingdom of God. Children are windows to heaven. So when we bring children to the Lord, we should be ready for him to teach us through them. Before the Lord we are all children. C. S. Lewis put it well: "When I became a man I put away childish things, including the fear of childishness and the desire to be very grown up."[4] This couple's experience reminded me that baptisms and dedications unite us all as children in need of our heavenly Father.

They also offer marvelous opportunities for teaching and witness. Though we have our respective orders of worship, here are some creative ideas used by pastors I know:

— Have the parents select appropriate Scripture passages to be read.

— Have a person other than the pastor pray for the child and family. Many times this will be a friend of the family or a relative. It can give godparents more than a superficial role in the spiritual nurture of the child. We recently had a service of dedication in which our guest preacher for the day happened to be a former seminary professor of one of the parents presenting a child. How stirring it was to hear this respected professor pray for the child of his former student.

— Use special music. Choirs can sing in preparation. So can soloists or ensembles. I've heard of gifted musicians composing songs to be sung during the ceremony. I'll never forget the day we had our children's choirs sing as the babies and their parents came forward.

— Other pastors have used selected poetry or prose, sometimes written for the occasion by a parent, relative, or family friend.

In either baptism or dedication, the same people who might be struggling to stay awake twenty minutes later during the sermon are now keenly alert. I try to seize the moment.

Faith in a Faithless World

Ours is a curious, tragic age. Children are both persecuted and pampered.

Articles on abortion, TV specials on abused children, and missing children staring at us from billboards and milk cartons remind us of our national epidemic of unwanted or mistreated children. As Christians we grieve over this plague and protest vigorously.

Yet we also live in a land that spends billions on designer clothes and high-tech accessories for our children. A recent article in *Time* noted: "Though parents pay the bills, precocious youngsters often insist on making decisions in matters of taste and style. . . . Notes a manager of Little Me in suburban Atlanta: 'The child comes in and says, "This is what I want. I won't wear anything else." These are very opinionated children.' . . . In fact, a well-dressed child may be the ultimate status symbol. . . . Observes a vice president at the advertising firm of Quinn and Johnson/BBDO, 'Kids are the BMWs of the '80s.' "[5]

This is the schizophrenic world into which we send our baptized and dedicated children. But as the old song says, "This world is not my home. I'm just a passin' through." These ancient Christian symbols provide roots in a rootless age. Both baptism and dedication boldly declare two foundational truths about the human condition.

First, these rites tell us we are sinners who need to be washed. Let's not be too sentimental. Regardless of the innocent beauty of children, they need redemption. I recall the comment of a seminary classmate when I asked how his eighteen-month-old baby was: "Well," he said, "original sin is alive and well."

Jesus invited the little children to come because he knew, better than anyone else, that they needed him, too.

And, second, when they came, he welcomed them with open arms. He is the waiting Father for all his prodigal sons and daughters. Baptism and dedication, therefore, not only declare our utter helplessness and need, but, because they point to Jesus Christ, also boldly proclaim "there is salvation in no one else, for there is no other name under heaven given among men by which we must be saved."[6]

Though we put proper focus on child, family, and church, Christ is the object. It is his story we tell. Every baptism and dedication demonstrates both hope and promise in that one true story. In a recent Christianity Today Institute, Dr. Donald Joy made the telling observation, "The faith is something that must be responded to individually. We can train. We can nurture. But they [the children] ultimately respond."[7]

Children of faith in a faithless world: our services of baptism and dedication proclaim a powerful alternative to a world that abuses children because "they get in my way" and indulges them because "they deserve the best." To the abandoned and abused children of our age, our services that enfold children shout with the voice of our Lord, "Stop! Do not hinder them. Let the little children come to me."

And for the pampered, preened, precocious children who are being taught the world revolves around them and their needs, baptism and dedication point to the Cross, and we hear these words: "Father, forgive them, for they know not what they do."

In the Chronicles of Narnia, C. S. Lewis gives a marvelous description of this two-fold proclamation: " 'You come of the Lord Adam and the Lady Eve,' said Aslan. 'And that is both honor enough to erect the head of the poorest beggar, and shame enough to bow the shoulders of the greatest emperor on earth.' "[8]

Pastoral words spoken and ministry given during the moments of baptism or dedication carry unusual weight. The infants are recipients. So are their parents. And the congregation not only hears the Story, but becomes part of it as they bring children to Christ.

When we ask the congregation to join in the nurture of the children before them, we are giving them a glorious privilege. It is no longer child or family alone against the world. God's people are now united, pilgrims together, passing on the faith to the next generation.

And I, as pastor, have been the sometimes-startled but always-awestruck master of ceremonies — ceremonies precious to our Lord.

---

1. Donald Bridge and David Phypers, *The Water That Divides* (Downers Grove, Ill.: InterVarsity Press, 1977), p. 7.

2. Frederick Buechner, *Wishful Thinking* (New York: Harper & Row, 1973), p. 6.

3. George Wither, poem published in *Hallelujah, or Britain's Second Remembrance*, 1660.

4. C. S. Lewis, *Of Other Worlds*, cited in Clyde S. Kilby, ed., *A Mind Awake* (New York: Harcourt, Brace & World, 1968), p. 32.

5. Gordon M. Henry, "High Fashion for Little Ones," *Time* (2 June 1986): 60.

6. Acts 4:12.

7. Donald Joy, quoted in "Building Faith: How a Child Learns to Love God," *Christianity Today* (13 June 1986): 15-I.

8. C. S. Lewis, *Prince Caspian* (New York: Collier, 1970), p. 212.

TWELVE

ADULT BAPTISMS

*Baptism must be seen near the heart of
our faith and presented as significant,
but not allowed to separate Christians
into groups of resentment or condescension. It must not become the "water that
divides us" but the water that witnesses
to our commitment to Christ.*

CALVIN MILLER

As a pastor, I like to envision myself as a great champion of the Christian faith. I have always thought it would be nice to die a martyr for some great theological truth — to gasp out my final breath for the ultimate victory of orthodoxy over classic Arianism.

However, I pastor in suburbia, where volleyball leagues get more attention than questions about Christ's deity. So most of the time I find my life given to more ordinary things. After all, most suburbanites can't understand why I take Christianity so seriously when there are sod webworms and dandelion epidemics.

Yet doctrinal issues are basic to faith, even in suburbia.

In today's world, one of my challenges as a pastor is dealing with "private faith" — people wanting a personal, but not visible, relationship with God. They like the security of feeling they know God, but they don't want anyone else to know they know him. They "accept Jesus," but reject demands to openly proclaim their allegiance.

Maybe this is one reason Jesus instructed his followers to make disciples and *baptize*. The doctrine of baptism is not just a damp aggravation Jesus tacked onto church practice to annoy those who come to faith. It is "an outward and visible sign of an inward and spiritual grace," an act of obedience, a public statement of faith.

Perhaps Jesus knew that a faith never publicly expressed had little chance of surviving. Certainly the church, throughout history, could not have survived unless believers had been willing to go public with their faith, even when it cost them their lives.

You'd expect a Baptist minister to say these things. What's interesting is that even in a Baptist church, many adults face the rite with a kind of terror. This terror is not so much a fear of drowning (though I have encountered even that) but a fear of being "center staged" and scrutinized as a new saint, a situation that can occur in any church — immersionist or not. Why this fear? There are several reasons.

Objections to Overcome

Leaving aside the theological debate about the mode of baptism for the moment, I find adults who come to Christ often object to baptism for three reasons.

First, the *adultness* of the person being baptized is a psychological stumbling block. There persists the feeling today that baptism is for children. The predominance of paedobaptism in our culture has no doubt accounted for this, but it is a widespread problem when adults come to faith. Clearing up this misunderstanding is work.

In terms of self-image, this reaction is understandable. I once took skiing lessons at a lodge in the Rockies. I felt foolish being the only adult in a class of preteens. I towered above them, often embarrassed that they did so much better than I was doing. I have tried to remember how I felt that afternoon as I attempt to explain to adult converts that baptism is not just kids' stuff.

Second, the *public nature* of baptism is troublesome to many. People often ask me if they could be baptized in some more private way. They would like it to be just me and them, or perhaps just a few friends. No amount of my reasoning has worked very well in overcoming this fear. I can point out theologically that baptism is an outward confession and would thus lose its meaning in a totally private service. Like a wedding, its great value is in its being seen — visible vows are vows of greater strength than those that are private and undisclosed.

It was because of this objection that I made baptism a part of our morning worship services. Part of the fear of a public baptism, I think, grew because many people were not familiar with the rite. Those who most needed it were not present at the Sunday evening services when it was usually practiced. By moving it to Sunday morning, it has become a regular part of worship and therefore is not seen as something of little importance, relegated to the secondary services.

As an immersionist, I've also found people unfamiliar and skeptical about the mode we practice. For those who have never seen it, or have only vague mental images of frontier revival meetings on the creek bank, the ceremony of baptism might appear unseemly, somehow not aesthetic enough to be a part of the dignity of morning worship. I've found these false notions are also removed by making baptism a regular part of morning worship.

Third, and closely related, is the obstacle of *vanity*. Baptism is, admittedly, an undignified experience, especially for those of us who immerse.

After I have introduced a new convert to Christ, I soon tell the person about baptism — often in the same visit during which the person confirmed his commitment to Christ. When people find out what I mean by baptism, they will often blurt out, "You mean under the water . . . in front of all those people?" They cannot imagine "the wet look" — make-up gone and hair style obliterated — in front of the whole congregation. For many people at such an imagined moment of horror, their theology collapses and psychology rises in protest.

Almost every adult convert will need help in all these areas. I've found it helpful to remember these are not theological attacks mounted by carnal converts. They are objections raised by self-image and natural self-esteem. All that is won spiritually can be lost psychologically.

The best, and most honest, way to overcome these objections, I believe, is to bring them out into the open. I gently let new converts know that fear is understandable. *Everybody* faces it. But there's more: to respond out of vanity when they have just given their entire lives to Christ is inconsistent. Dignity has its place, but it cannot be allowed to supplant a daring decision.

As one who practices immersion, I face yet another obstacle, a practical one: immersion is simply more physical than drier forms of baptism. Many heavier adults look at their minister and doubt. These may need a little assurance that the minister is able to perform all he would ask of them.

I have never quite decided if I did the right thing with Zelpha Ettinger. Zelpha came into full relationship with Christ, but weighing over two hundred fifty pounds, she eyed my thin frame with suspicion.

"Do you think you can do it?" she asked.

I assured her I could, but she, in tears, asked if I would fill the baptistery on a Tuesday and baptize her with no one in the sanctuary so she would know for sure I could do it later with the whole congregation present. So I did. The practice session, I must confess, healed my doubts as well as hers.

I remember Julie Thompson, who was far less heavy than Zelpha, but she was proud that I had baptized her, too, with such grace. She would often introduce me to her family and friends as "My pastor . . . who baptized even me." I always felt like the Rev. Schwarzenegger as she proudly told her friends of my ability to baptize even the more beefy converts.

Perhaps it's good, in such moments, to be able to laugh at what we are, but to remember also that Jesus did indeed call us to go into all the world and teach the gospel to every creature, baptizing them in the name of the Father, the Son and the Holy Spirit. Knowing how much we want to see all the world's people baptized into the faith, perhaps God can forgive our lack of dignity.

I try not to be defensive, but I sometimes feel that immersion receives more of the brunt of jibe and satire in popular imagination than the simpler modes of baptism. I earlier alluded to the stereotype of the "overalls and farm pond" congregations singing "Shall We Gather at the River," which has left our perceived image somewhere closer to dusty back roads than today's chrome-and-glass offices where our custom can appear quaint and out-of-date. Perhaps the hillbilly look of the ordinance contributes to the fear of the water.

I remember one stylish young woman in my first church who came to a personal faith in Jesus Christ. Soon after, I began to talk to her about baptism. She was horrified at the idea. (She had never heard of the rite and was shocked just to know of its existence, let alone her own need of it to become a member of our church.) She never said immersion was rural and plain, yet her reluctance said it for her. It was many weeks before she finally agreed to be baptized.

And if a person doesn't have personal fears, often the attitudes of other people present obstacles. For instance, teenagers may face baptism under the jocular sway of parents who attend their baptism service but joke about their child's "dunking" or "swimming lesson," thus implying the whole service is silly or undignified. The richness is stolen from the occasion, and a child may feel a kind of flippant rejection of that which he or she has taken so seriously.

Steps from Conversion to Baptism

In this brief section, it should be understood, I give but one man's way, developed across twenty-five years and two thousand baptisms. In baptizing an average of two people a week, I have discovered the importance of gentleness, patience, and thorough explanation concerning baptism.

The vast majority of those two thousand people were adults.

The vigor and enthusiasm of the newly baptized has infused our church with energy. Still I speak cautiously, because every pastor ministers uniquely, especially with new converts. But let me describe the steps I try to take between conversion and immersion.

The first step, even with new converts, is to be open about my baptismal practices. I have instructed our staff and the scores of lay people trained to evangelize that as soon as anyone comes to faith in Christ, we should mention baptism and the relationship of the ritual to the faith they have just professed. There is, of course, some risk of losing a new convert by going too quickly to the matter of baptism. But I feel the risk must be taken so that the convert sees the relationship of his new-found Lord to all of life in the church, beginning with public profession of faith in Christ — and baptism.

This up-front presentation prevents a feeling of being "swindled" by a quick and easy presentation of the gospel that must later be amended by secondary requirements. This feeling is not unlike the one when you purchase a new automobile and find at the cash register that the purchase price does not include a thousand dollar's worth of options as well as preparation and delivery costs.

The second step is undelayed enrollment in a New Christians' Class. We want new converts to understand how belief in Christ fits with baptism, Communion, and all the other aspects of discipleship. We offer the classes before church on Sunday mornings because it is the one time each week when the most people can attend. Sunday night attendance is less easily motivated, and week nights present an unbelievable set of scheduling conflicts.

I'll admit to the downside of this approach. New converts have as great a need to belong as they do to be instructed. Membership in a New Christians' Class helps with the necessary instruction, but if Sunday school classes are the basis for fellowship and belonging in your church, it can frustrate the new Christian's need to get involved in a group of other Christians. Therefore, we limit the length of the instruction to only a few weeks to avoid excessive segregation from the larger group.

The third step is to make sure that our church, in arranging for the baptism, is courteous and willing to keep the converts well informed. The convert will want to know all the details. We mail letters that spell out when and where to meet the pastor before the service, and what to bring (including towels, dry undergarments, and hair dryers). Early in the week of the baptism, we mail a second letter that again covers the facts and confirms their participation.

The fourth step of preparation is a gentle reminder of everyone's right to dignity. I have long believed that to ask anyone to undress in full view of others can impose a terrible kind of indignity, especially for children or those who are shy. In both the men's dressing room and the women's, we have provided partitions to keep anyone from having to undress in front of others.

The fifth step is the briefing I hold with participants fifteen minutes before the service. It's my last-minute but special time with the new converts. Here we rehearse the procedure: how to enter the baptistery and leave it, the importance of handrails, reading each candidate's name in the order of the baptism, introducing those who are helping in the dressing rooms. Finally, we go through a dry run, showing the candidates exactly what I will say and what they will say. I fully explain the procedure, asking one of the candidates to serve as a model for the others, showing how I will hold them during the rite and how I will call them to the water and send them from it.

Then I pray with the group, holding hands. This prayer celebrates the importance of what they are doing and points to the spiritual meaning of the event. It's one of the most important things I do. For one thing, it reminds us all of the spiritual significance of the event. So many times, the dressing rooms are filled with nervous or light chit-chat that robs the event of its spiritual tone. This brief prayer time helps us focus on the meaning of what we're doing.

It also serves a second purpose. This prayer can allay some of the natural fears of those about to be baptized. It provides a time of peace in a nervous and dyspeptic time. The timid feel uncomfortable with all they are being asked to do and say before so many people. Prayer brings a sense of community to the group. It is difficult to feel alone as you pray with others who are going through the same feelings of fear and inadequacy.

The last step that needs to be remembered is that, whether or not the church requires a testimony from the baptistery, the event is an act of worship. We use Scripture, organ, lighting, and even choral responses with the ordinance. When married couples are baptized, we like to include them both in the baptistery at the same time. Even whole families may be baptized at once. The appropriate Scripture before or after the baptism of a child, engaged couple, family, or single parent can enhance the event and make it more worshipful and memorable.

The presentation of baptismal certificates can be done formally or informally, publicly or privately, but we have them already typed and signed before the baptism begins.

We've found that with these procedures, the fears that often surround baptism can be diminished, even eliminated.

Baptism must be allowed to live near the heart of our faith, without fear, whatever form it takes. It must be seen and presented as significant, without allowing it to separate Christians into groups of resentment or condescension. It must not become the "water that divides us" but the water that witnesses to our commitment to Christ. It demonstrates that our submission to the New Testament, which has few rites for us to practice, should not be abandoned simply because there are different views on how the rite is to be practiced.

Above all, baptism must stand for basic truth as well as a greatness of spirit. It reminds us who have undergone the water that we are to serve one another in love and welcome all into the arms of relationship with Christ.

THIRTEEN

CONFIRMATION

A vital confirmation service begins long before that Sunday in late spring.

PAUL ANDERSON

Confirmation class has been defined as "that time of the week when the pastor questions his call to ministry."

I remember my father, a pastor, grumbling that "these kids want to attend catechism class about as much as they want to sit in school." I never appreciated my father's feelings until I became a pastor and, sitting in the middle of a confirmation classroom, began to consider seriously my aptitude for selling insurance. Not that the time was a complete loss. I learned a great deal — that the epistles are the wives of the apostles, for example, or that Martin Luther King is Martin Luther's brother.

Frustrations like these led folks at Trinity Lutheran to retool our entire confirmation process, from the first parents' orientation meeting to the close of the confirmation service. After overseeing the new program for twelve years, I'm still amazed how a few key principles transform what could be a downer into a delight.

Get 'em Early

We're all agreed that a vital confirmation experience begins long before that Sunday in late spring when the nervous confirmands stand before the congregation. That's why we start early with years of classroom instruction. But at Trinity we found we weren't starting early enough.

Most teenagers are convinced that confirmation is a bad idea. The only way a pastor has half a chance is to reach kids before they become teenagers and hear from their peers, "Aw, confirmation is a bummer."

So we go after kids in the fourth grade. The children proceed through three years of instruction during fourth, fifth, and sixth grades and then have a year of transition and service in their seventh-grade year, with confirmation that spring.

Too early? You should see how eager these fourth graders are. They tug on your arm in August and announce, "I get to start confirmation this year." For them confirmation means honor, not boredom.

Last fall my son Andrew started the confirmation process. Andrew and I went to the orientation meeting and sat with the other fourth graders and parents. The lay people who led our program passed out the workbooks the youngsters would be using during the year and walked them through a few sample assignments. As I already knew, a good degree of each lesson was mechanical: underlining key statements in the biblical text, marking symbols to show contrasts, identifying the passage's main idea. My son looked it all over, then blurted out, "Hey, this is going to be fun!"

Fourth graders' hearts are usually still tender toward the gospel. They have had fewer years of indoctrination in a worldly system of thought that resists spiritual penetration. They are less influenced by peers, who in a few years might try telling them that religion is nowhere. And they are equipped to handle the spiritual concepts we teach. We've found we tend to underestimate their abilities rather than overestimate them. They are more ready to grapple with truth then we are to challenge them with it.

Beyond Teaching to Training

While teaching informs, training forms. Our best teaching means little if we don't train children to live what they learn.

We want them to not only know Bible truths but to live Bible lives. So we spend as much time on application as we do on information.

In one unit, the students wrote a play on the miracles of Jesus and then presented it in a convalescent home. For a lesson on prejudice, students interviewed the local newspaper editor about where prejudice is at work in our community and asked our church president about prejudice in our church. Following a lesson on service, classes have washed windows for church members and sometimes have cleaned my office.

Training also means we establish a relationship with students. At Trinity, students and teachers meet for dinner before class. Talking about the lesson during dinner is off-limits. We talk about what went on in school, skateboarding, fun times they've had lately.

Having said that, however, we know we can't violate sound educational principles and hope to succeed. Our confirmation teachers go through a four-session course to refine teaching skills. We try to pair each beginning teacher with a seasoned one. This gives the less-experienced person a valuable apprenticeship, lightens the workload of each person, and keeps the class going even when one teacher can't make it. With two teachers in the classroom, we've had fewer problems keeping classes quiet and orderly.

In the classroom, teachers use lecture sparingly and try to incorporate drama, games, word exercises, songs, and other more innovative approaches. In one unit, for example, a student put the life of Abraham into a rhyming story. For a lesson on heaven, a class threw a "Heavenly Festival," including a time of worship and angel food cake for refreshments. Our goal is not to entertain, but what we teach is so important that we want to teach it as winsomely as we can.

Keep Them Involved

We, like many churches, have struggled with how to integrate students into the youth group and the life of the church following their years of instruction. Some families have inherited the understanding that the confirmation service ends the child's obligation to the church.

Because we don't want to usher children out of the church with confirmation, we inserted a year of transition and service after the children complete their studies and before they are confirmed. During this year we encourage the kids to be involved regularly in worship and youth group activities, and we try to involve them in service. We've had these young people baby-sit for new members' classes, clean the building, and set up tables and movie projectors for church events.

We want confirmation to serve as the launching pad for service in the congregation. Before last spring's confirmation service, one young man told me he couldn't wait for confirmation because he wanted to be doing more in the congregation.

But to be honest, we have yet to structure a truly effective program for this transition year. We're convinced the idea is a good one; we just need more stick-to-itiveness to make it work fully.

Work with the Parents

Martin Luther wrote the *Small Catechism* to help parents teach their children the key points of Christian doctrine. We do not want to supercede parents in this primary role, but assist them.

At the orientation meeting, we ask parents to work with their children on the lessons, which come on both Wednesday nights and during Sunday school. Some families have chosen to use the lessons for their family devotions. The program is rigorous, and parents usually breathe a deep sigh of relief when the three years are over, but they feel good being part of a job well done. One couple, whose three young-adult boys still talk about their confirmation experience, smiled as they told me, "We huffed and puffed our way through catechism."

Parents have also been drawn into the interview process

preceding the formal confirmation service. Until a few years ago, the pastor was the only one to interview the student to determine whether he or she was ready to be confirmed. But who knows the child better than his or her parents?

Once I interviewed a young person prior to confirmation and afterward told him I had some concerns about his readiness. Later his parents, who had another son in the program, came to see me. "If you had said this about our other son," they said, "we would agree. But we know our boys, and this one is more ready than the other. He's quiet and not as articulate, but he has a genuine faith."

So now parents interview their children first and then give me a brief written report that I may use as material in my own interview with the child the following month. I write a letter to the parents and suggest questions they may want to use in their personal conference with the child. The questions range widely but focus on the child's growing commitment to Christ. For example, one question I often suggest is, "When have you felt closest to God?"

Many parents have told me this conversation is one of the most meaningful they've had with their children. They also tell me it's not easy. One strong supporter of our program admitted, "That was hard work."

Finally, parents are involved in the confirmation service itself. I invite them to come forward and participate in the prayers that accompany the laying on of hands. Then the parents and confirmands form the first table for Communion.

Add the Personal Touch

The day before Confirmation Sunday, I meet with the parents and the children. I have two goals for this time. I want to prepare them to feel as comfortable as possible during the service and understand what's happening. I also want this time to add a personal touch, to seal my pastoral contact with them.

I usually review "Why confirmation?" and explain this is

not an end but a beginning, parallel to Jesus beginning his ministry after his confirmation at the Jordan. I explain what the youth are confirming — their faith in Jesus Christ, that they will live in the covenant of their baptism. I encourage them to expect that the Holy Spirit will do some confirming as well. As we pray in the service, "Father in heaven, for Jesus' sake, stir up in your child the gift of your Holy Spirit; confirm his faith, guide his life, empower him in his serving, give him patience in suffering, and bring him to everlasting life."

Then I walk the children and parents through the service so they know what's coming. Afterward, I invite all the kids to my house for lunch. I take time to talk with each one. During my conversation, I refresh my memory about their interests, hobbies, family situations. The next day, when the confirmands come forward during the service, I use this information to introduce each one personally: "This is Ryan Hoffman. Ryan really enjoys skateboarding. Ryan feels God may be calling him to be a missionary. Let's pray for him in that regard." Then I have each child share a portion of Scripture that has been especially meaningful to him or her. This also allows the congregation to get to know the young person better.

Another personal touch comes when we invite the parents forward to join in the prayers that accompany the laying on of hands. It's so moving to hear parents pray for their children. Sometimes parents will say a few words to their son or daughter during this time. I recall one father saying to his daughter, "You have been such a fine, obedient girl. We really love you and believe God has a special plan for you." Last year one child's grandmother came forward to pray for her grandson. We were all deeply touched by her prayer.

I've found that these personal touches in the prayers, Scriptures, and prophetic words are what people remember most.

Weighing the Trade-offs

Our approach to confirmation has come with a price. For this church, building a strong confirmation program meant gathering a crew of adults to be teachers, cooks for the weekly supper, administrators, table hostesses, and so on. The price was the loss of our strong choir. When we began our new program, the choir dropped out of existence. We've had choirs since, but not with the same level of involvement.

We had to weigh the trade-offs. We feel the gains in our situation outweigh the losses. The team-teaching approach means we have trained dozens of teachers in the process of training our youth. The biblical literacy of our congregation has risen considerably. Relationships between young people and adults remain vital. In fact, young people tell me their favorite activity is our annual family retreat.

The students have more confidence reading the Scriptures; they are not intimidated by obscure minor prophets. They have discovered the Bible speaks to their lives and helps them live more wisely. And they have built long-lasting friendships with the other children in the program.

Confirmation may cause some of us to question our calling, but with the right approach, I've found it actually confirms mine.

FOURTEEN

SPEAKING BEFORE THE COMMUNITY

I will never again assume that quasi *has to describe my declaration of the gospel at religious gatherings in the community.*

CAL LEMON

One of my fears in seminary was that the watching world would peg me as "Mr. Mush Minister." You know the type — in commercials when the script calls for a little sanctimonious sentimentality, they drag out this middle-aged, balding wimp with wire-rimmed glasses and a benign smile.

Well that's not me. I may be middle-aged and balding, but I can't be sold to the highest bidder who needs a little God for an otherwise undivine life. I can't see straight when I get the impression someone wants to use me.

That means I have a problem: "being used" is part of the job description of the ministry.

Let me explain. I'm convinced that everyone, sinner or saint, thinks he needs a little of God. Even to many un-churched, the mention of God, by someone who speaks for God, can usher in great comfort. And comfort is part of our portfolio. As much as I loathe the implications, in my community I'm probably viewed by some as God, Jr.

And as God, Jr., I am often invited to say some God words at community functions so people will feel better about their eating, voting, football playing, graduating, or grocery store opening.

Though my pride may protest this apparent prostituting of piety, I have to realize that people have asked to hear God through me. Even though our communities often see us as pallid stand-ins for an absentee God, we can seize these public platforms to play out grace. Grace will get a hearing, not because of our black suits or FM "easy listening" voices, but because grace is God's line — and everyone knows that.

So bring on God, Jr. Even as a stand-in, I get to recite the original script.

Designated Prayer

In my ministry, one of the first places I was asked to stand in for God was saying grace at a Kiwanis luncheon. There I was, standing behind a beer-stained podium in a basement restaurant that smelled like low tide at Coney Island. The Kiwanis president rang the bell, told an off-color joke, and slapped me on the back, saying, "Okay, Reverend, give us a good one." The hush that came over the crowd was anything but holy.

"Lord," I started, "it's been a busy day for most of us, and we have to admit we are just a little taken aback to be talking to you right now. As a matter of fact, Lord, most of us haven't thought about you in a long, long time. . . ." I decided to go for broke, putting my money on honesty. When the traditional amen sounded in the smoke-filled air, for at least ten seconds, no one moved or spoke. It was then I realized people actually could hear God's voice when mine had spoken.

That Kiwanis grace has established for me some specific principles that I follow when praying in public settings:

First, I never use Elizabethan English, religious jargon, or biblical references. That shoptalk only alienates people and reinforces unbelievers' worst fear: the faithful are a holy club.

Second, I specifically mention the personality of the audience. If I'm praying at a Thanksgiving assembly for school-age children, I may say, "Lord, you know how hard it will be for us to wait to pray before we dig in on Thursday."

Third, I keep prayers short. When people start counting the tiles around their chairs, I have prayed too long. The spiritual attention span of a nonchurch audience is profoundly short, so I limit the length of my prayers.

Fourth, if I write out a prayer before the event, I memorize it. When the audience sees a printed prayer unfolding from my pocket, they assume they're going to get a speech with heads bowed. I want people to know I'm talking to God, and I fear that won't come through if I'm looking at a crib sheet.

Fifth, above all else, I direct my prayer to God. If prayer is used as a bulletin board for tacking some direct messages to my audience, my spiritual credibility is undermined.

People see us for who we are, but they will also see more in us than we, in ourselves, have to offer. I have to remind myself constantly that prayer is intimate, face-to-face communication with Divinity. I'm convinced that if I'm honest with God speaking on behalf of the audience, sincerity is picked up by my listeners. They are witnessing a divine-human dialogue. No one will count linoleum tiles when that dynamic transpires.

Special Events

Another setting where God, Jr., is often invited to make an appearance is the national quasireligious event. Memorial Day, Martin Luther King's birthday, Veterans Day, Brotherhood Week, and high school baccalaureate services all call for large doses of clergy.

These occasions provide us some distinct advantages over, say, offering the invocation at the grand opening of a convenience store. The public comes relatively primed for some piety; part of the purpose of these special events is to be culturally religious.

I have had both good and bad experiences with the high school baccalaureate service. I'll begin with the bad.

It was a rural high school on a very hot Sunday afternoon in early June. The kids marched in to Vivaldi, but it was obvious that Madonna and Mr. Mister were beating out some silent refrain in their brains. The parents were perched in bleacher seats preparing their spines for the chiropractor on Monday morning. That stuffy gymnasium contained all the makings for a religious bomb, and I turned out to be the main ingredient.

I winged my remarks. "You are the future leaders of America," I began. "America, a country crying out for moral giants . . ." It got worse from there, I must confess. The students fidgeted and giggled over the creative uses they devised for their bulletins. The parents nodded off into a sweaty slumber. I realized I was a dud with more fizzle than sizzle. I had not anticipated how hard I would have to work to capture this audience.

Long before they arrived, I later realized, the kids had decided the only reason they were there was for their parents. The parents had hauled their kids before me, it seems, to fill some desperate, guilt-assuaging need to "give them everything I can afford." God is affordable, so religious services at commencement time are, in my opinion, religious barbiturates that parents gulp down to handle another stage of separation anxiety.

Well, after receiving the pleasant smiles of assuaged parents and the yawns of their children, I vowed, if ever given the chance again, to alter drastically my approach to baccalaureate services. Two years later I got that second chance.

As I considered the previous disaster, I decided I had to invest in either the kids or the parents. I failed the last time partially because I had tried to hit both and ended up hitting neither. So for this message, I chose the kids.

After my introduction, I strode briskly to the front of the stage (I had the podium removed before the service started) and said, "In 1983 your world staggered under the weight of war in the Middle East and famine in Ethiopia, but you swayed to the happiness of 'Footloose.' " Under these opening lines rose the narcotic music of Bonnie Tyler's "I Need a Hero" from the movie's hit album. I stopped speaking for about a minute while the sound technician brought up the music to teeth-rattling volume.

I had them.

For the next twenty minutes, I spoke to those teenagers about their world — filled with pastel "jams," Donkey Kong video games, and the riches of Lionel Richie. I talked about the need for heroes and the haunts where we search for them. Then I zeroed in on Tyler's lyrics, "I need a hero, bigger than life . . . straight from the fight." The Christ-figure had been set up for me.

The beat of the song crescendoed to end the presentation — but not the thoughts. I have been astounded that two years later I'm still running into people at restaurants and grocery stores who remember the theme of that short message.

I will never again assume that *quasi* has to describe my declaration of the gospel at religious gatherings in the community. I'm not looking for decisions, but I can expect responses to grace, regardless of the spiritual history of the audience. I've found I have to approach these events with more prayer and study than I do preaching on Sunday. I have to work as hard knowing the world in my audience as I do the Word in my study. Then I have to commit my presentation to memory so that all my body is focused on the listener as I try to communicate sacred truth to secular minds.

I try beforehand to talk with people who normally attend these yearly functions to update my character sketch of the audience. I arrange a short tour of the auditorium, gymnasium, or amphitheater to get a feel for the physical setting from several different directions. That allows me to visualize myself from the audience's perspective.

Finally, I work to be specific, with myself and my audience, about what I hope to accomplish when I leave my seat on the platform and command their attention. Since I don't want to waste anybody's time or my opportunity, the extra time I take to make an occasion work is well spent.

The Media Man

Probably the most threatening appearance for God, Jr., is with the media. Each statement is so public and final.

I write on a word processor. My computer, next to God and

my dog, is the most forgiving entity in my life. With the press of a *Control W*, I can wipe out a word, sentence, or paragraph. If I'm nauseated with the whole composition, I can hit *Control N* to erase everything and start with a blank screen. *Control N* is my favorite key.

There are no *Control N*s in media. In parish ministry, if we create yawns one Sunday, we know the faithful will be back next week to give us another crack. With the media, however, our words, gestures, emotions, and theology cannot be retrieved, scrubbed, and tried again.

This finality of media often intimidates us, but I don't want to forfeit a useful channel for the communication of truth. I do have misgivings about the electronic church and what it may be saying to the watching world, and I don't recommend establishing another college, amusement park, or forest of satellite dishes. But I believe the media can communicate spiritual life.

Radio. Here is a medium that television was supposed to have buried long ago. Instead, statistics prove that almost 85 percent of the American public listens to the radio at least once every day. For clergy, radio offers several options.

First, the news departments of many radio stations are scrambling to find suitable community leaders to give responses to social and ethical issues. Pastors who introduce themselves to the station managers are mentally logged for future reference.

Second, radio is interested in audience participation. Since radio activates the imagination, the forum format is still very popular. It is not overly forward to call and offer yourself as a guest on a "talk radio" station. Radio producers are constantly scratching for new ideas and people.

While pastoring in Boston, I was a guest on a talk show that reached half a million people. The agnostic host pressed me on the question, "What does it mean to be *born again?*" We received such a visceral response from the listening audience that our one-hour segment ran three. Back home in my living room after the broadcast was over, I realized all the things I didn't say or said wrong, but I took great comfort in knowing I had said something. Being there, I believe, is what God is asking of us in the use of this medium.

A third way to utilize radio is through "on-air commentaries." Because both radio and television are required by the Federal Communications Commission to provide a certain amount of "public service time," stations are looking for competent writers who are able to make a point succinctly.

Television. With the advent of cable television, there are myriad possibilities for our communities to know us and to know what we believe, but they will not come looking for us. It will take an aggressive communicator of the Word to find these free and open opportunities on television. In Cambridge, Massachusetts, with only twenty-four people in our church, we produced a television show with a "video magazine" format that the Boston station liked so much they offered us a weekly time slot — and paid me to produce it! It can be done by an ordinary church.

My only word of caution is: Don't allow the medium to corrupt your motives. When we see our likenesses on that screen, personal kingdom building easily becomes a lust. But we shouldn't turn off to the idea of God using this medium because of that face on the screen.

Newspapers. Ever since Johann Gutenberg imprinted that first piece of paper, the world has never been the same. Those who think what is lying on the front lawn at 6 A.M. is only good for lining shelves haven't fully understood the power of print. Millions of people, even in an age when satellites dish up the news with microsecond speed, carefully turn every page, foraging for the right words — words that cajole, excite, and inform. The black smudges of printers' ink still tattoo the hands of many.

Newspapers are looking for people — not to join their staff, but to write well. Most papers don't care as much about the position we take as our effectiveness in communicating it. I've regularly written for our local paper's opinion section. I write and rewrite and rewrite again until I can sleep with my words.

I am astounded by the many people in my community who forage through my syntax looking for truth.

Most newspapers have a religion editor. I suggest making an appointment with this person. Make it nothing more than a courtesy call. In that conversation you will establish yourself as a resource when he or she writes a local story on the religious community. You may find this editor calling you from time to time for some quotable quotes on a particular subject like the political clout of the Religious Right, or faith healing. If you don't think fast on your receiver, ask to call back in a few moments with a response after you have had time to think. Most editors don't work on "hold the presses" margins. They will be happy to have your input.

It may seem egotistical, but pastors can make an impact on their communities by sending out press releases listing the places they serve outside their churches. If they chair a committee to restore low-income housing or are speaking at a district gathering, the community should know. That information may give unchurched people the freedom to trust them, and that trust may extend someday into accepting His story through your story.

If we are content to cloister ourselves in our kingdoms and Kittels, we haven't yet proclaimed the Good News of the gospel. Sure, the congregation pays the salary, but the community is our parish. And special occasions in our communities become prime occasions to interject a timely word for God.